P9-BYE-218

honey

by **Stephanie Rosenbaum**

photographs by **Caroline Kopp**

honey

from flower to table

* * *

CHRONICLE BOOKS

SAN FRANCISCO

Text copyright © 2002 by Stephanie Rosenbaum

Photographs copyright © 2002 by Caroline Kopp

Library of congress cataloging-in-publication data available.

ISBN: 0-8118-3238-4

Printed in Singapore

Designed by Efrat Rafaeli

Prop styling by Carol Hacker

Food and craft styling by Clair Hadley

The photographer would like to thank beekeepers Spencer and Helene Marshall
of Marshall's Farm, and Hector Alvarez of Hector's Apiares Services for their time and generosity.
Many thanks to Tom Chester, Irene Davidson, Joe Guliane, and Yvonne Johnson at the
San Francisco Beekeepers' Association. Thanks also to Helie Robertson for her lovely garden,
and Karen and Tim Bates from The Apple Farm for their beautiful orchard.

Distributed in Canada by Raincoast Books
9050 Shaughnessy Street, Vancouver, British Columbia V6P 6E5

10 9 8 7 6 5 4 3 2 1

Chronicle Books LLC
85 Second Street, San Francisco, California 94105
www.chroniclebooks.com

✳ ✳ ✳ ✳ ✳

acknowledgments

Many thanks to Flo Braker, Elizabeth Faulkner, Fran Gage, David Lebowitz, Mani Niall, James Ormsby, and Tori Ritchie for their advice, culinary expertise, and honey lore. Beekeepers Tom Chester and Robert MacKimmie, along with others from the San Francisco Beekeepers' Association and the staff of the San Francisco League of Urban Gardeners, provided a wealth of information about getting started with bees. Many thanks to Helene and Spencer Marshall of Marshall's Farm for sharing their passion for Bay Area honey, and to the National Honey Board for all their useful information.

I would like to thank my editor at Chronicle Books, Mikyla Bruder, for her patience, support, and great ideas, and for the careful work of assistant editor Jodi Davis, copy editor Deborah Bruce, and design coordinator Azi Rad. I am indebted to designer Efrat Rafaeli and photographer Caroline Kopp for their beautiful work on this book.

My personal thanks also go to Paige Rogers for bringing me honey from around the globe; to Charlotte Rogers Melrose for her recipe-testing assistance; to Jennifer Joseph for sharing challah, advice, and trips to farmers' markets; to Brian Bouldrey for his useful information on Catholicism and the Masons; and to Joy Connolly at Stanford University for Greek and Roman honey customs.

To my mother, Leslie Faulds, for her unstinting love, encouragement, and honey challah recipes, and to my father, Jack Rosenbaum, for sharing his lifelong love of food and writing.

And to Eric, for making my life so sweet.

* * * * *

table of contents

I have gathered my myrrh with my spice;
I have eaten my honeycomb with my honey . . .

Song of Songs

introduction

The Owl and the Pussycat sailed with it. John the Baptist lived on it. Alexander the Great was buried in it. Philosophers, poets, and popes have exalted it. And a certain chubby bear of "very little brain" was tempted into many sticky situations by the promise of a jar of it. Magically created by bees out of the nectar of flowers; food for gods, saints, peasants, and kings, honey has occupied a central place in culinary and cultural history for thousands of years. Would the Israelites have made it through forty years in the desert on the promise of a land awash only in milk?

What would a wedding be without a honeymoon? Or a hot biscuit without a voluptuous golden puddle oozing out of every buttery bite? Honey can turn lemons into lemonade, sweeten a cup of tea, soothe a sore throat, cure hay fever, purify a wound, energize a sprinter, and keep a cake moist for days. (And preserve a severed head, but that's another story.) Rich in metaphor, the story of honey is a fascinating one, spanning centuries and dipping into myth, religion, science, poetry, and literature.

Freshly broken from the hive, a chunk of new honeycomb is ripe with all the intoxicating sweetness of a summer day. Veiled in this fragile filigree of wax is the essence of sunshine, golden and limpid, tasting of grassy meadows, mountain wildflowers, lavishly blooming orange trees, or scrubby desert weeds. Honey, even more than wine, is a reflection of place. If the process of grape to glass is alchemy, then the trail from blossom to bottle is one of reflection. The nectar collected by the bee is the spirit and sap of the plant, its sweetest juice. Honey is the flower transmuted, its scent and beauty transformed into aroma and taste.

Authentic, unadulterated, and pure, honey is the only sweetener in nature that can be eaten just as it comes. For bees, the history of honey stretches back over millions of years, as does their intensely social way of living. The production of the hexagonal honeycomb; the three-tier community of queen, drones, and workers; the transformation of flower nectar into honey—all these were in place long before even our most ancient records. Yet anyone with curiosity, a backyard, and a modicum of equipment can tap into the wealth of this fertile tradition. In fact, with so much of the population of wild bees decimated by loss of habitat, pesticides, and a deadly, widespread epidemic of varroa mites, keeping bees is not only fun and productive but ecologically sound. And just as the happiest gardeners are those who let the plants' needs dictate the style of the garden, keeping bees successfully is all about letting the bees teach you what they require. No matter how much honey, beeswax, pollen, propolis, and royal jelly a beekeeper reaps from his or her hives, it's the bees that really know how a beehive should be run. As Ozark beekeeper Sue Hubbell notes in her apiary journal, *A Book of Bees,* "The only time I ever believed that I knew all there was to know about beekeeping was the first year I was keeping them. Every year since, I've known less and less and have accepted the humbling truth that bees know more about making honey than I do."

From across the United States and around the world, a growing interest in artisanal honeys has revived the ancient art of small-scale beekeeping. While commercial blends of clover and wildflower honey are reliable and easy to find in any supermarket, curious honey lovers can now find dozens of exotic honeys for sale, from creamy, snow-white Hawaiian honey to teak-colored Italian chestnut honey. Sage and mesquite honeys are prized in the American West, as is tupelo honey in the South, buckwheat in the Midwest, blueberry and cranberry in the Northeast, and eucalyptus, manzanita, and star thistle along the Pacific coast. Like fine wine or freshly pressed olive oil, honey reflects the taste of its source, and each harvest is unique.

So come and get your fingers sticky. The sun is high, the bees are humming, and somewhere, a fragrant flower is just unfolding its petals to the breeze.

chapter 1

honey in history
and the
history of honey

Thus may we gather honey from the weed,
And make a moral of the devil himself.

William Shakespeare,
Henry V, *act 4, scene 1*

History is rich in honey lore. While honeybees began, some fifty million years ago, as solitary insects, it was their evolution into centralized honey-producing societies that led to their inextricable connection to human development.

Apis mellifera, the common or Western honeybee, is native to Africa, Europe, and the Middle East. Other *Apis* varieties, including *A. dorsata, A. florea,* and *A. cerana,* developed in Asia. In Central and South America, honey was produced only by the native stingless bees (genus *Melipona*) until the arrival of European honeybees with Western explorers in the late fifteenth century.

Scientists estimate that honey found its way into the human diet some two to three million years ago. At a time when securing sufficient nourishment required a perilous mixture of risk, danger, and luck, a cache of honeycomb must have seemed like a gift from the gods. Besides its remarkable sweetness, honey was a food unsurpassed in energy value. Composed of nearly 75 percent easily digestible sugars, with valuable trace vitamins and minerals, honey was a perfect addition to a rough diet. Besides honey, the comb provided protein in the form of immature bee grubs (larvae) and stored pollen.

Starting around 10,000 B.C. prehistoric peoples started recording their experiences tracking honey to its source. In Bicorp, Spain, a Stone Age cave painting dated to approximately 7000 B.C. depicts a small figure on a ladder propped up against a cliff face, collecting honeycomb into a pot or basket while surrounded by clouds of bees. Known as bee hunting, this way of harvesting honey would persist throughout the world, from medieval Germany to tribal Africa, tropical Asia to twentieth-century rural Appalachia.

Mindful of natural predators, particularly bears, wild bees rarely choose easily accessible places in which to nest, preferring hollows found in tall trees or rocky cliffs. The unpredictability of finding consistently rich natural hives to rob made bee hunting a precarious means of supplying this precious food. If honey was to keep pace with societies increasingly geared above the level of mere subsistence, it, like other agricultural products, had to come under human control.

The earliest evidence of beekeeping, as opposed to bee hunting, appears in Egypt at approximately 2400 B.C. Rather than going to the bees, the Egyptians learned that the bees could be brought to them. Since *A. mellifera* was a nesting bee, living in multicombed structures built inside dark, enclosed spaces (unlike *A. dorsata* and *A. florea*, whose colonies live along a single strip of comb built in the open air and so cannot be hived), the Egyptians discovered that, once captured, a swarm of bees could easily be coerced into taking up residence in a long, cylindrical pipe rather than a hollow tree.

To hold their bees, the Egyptians constructed horizontal hives of sun-hardened clay or mud pipes, which were stacked alongside and on top of one another. An entrance hole at the front of the pipe served as a front door for the bees; at the back, a larger hole allowed the beekeeper to remove the comb as needed. This dual entrance method prevented the beekeeper from getting in the way of the bees on their foraging flights. Bees are notoriously single-minded when flying in search of nectar. As anyone who has watched a hive in full swing can attest, bees really do make a direct beeline from flower to hive, and any obstacle that prevents easy access to the hive is likely to get stung. The front entrance to the hive would also be the one protected by the colony's guard bees, who would be on the lookout for any predators trying to rob the hive. Entering from the back and shielded by the wall of hives, the keeper was much less likely to get stung, especially if he had smoked the hive in advance.

To smoke a hive, paper, bark, hay, or twine is stuffed into a container (now commonly a metal can) and set alight. Then, using a small bellows, smoke from the smoldering materials is gently puffed into the hive. Believing their home to be in danger, perhaps from a nearby forest fire, the bees rush to pack food (that is, honey) into their stomachs in case a sudden exodus becomes necessary. Thus engaged, they are too busy to heed any two-legged invaders. (Another theory holds that smoking results in bees too full to sting: with their stomachs so engorged, they can't bend into the position necessary for stinging.)

Once gathered, honeycomb was kept in shallow, covered pottery dishes; examples of these, some with pollen grains or fragments of wax intact, have been found in Egyptian tombs. Beekeeping was so much a part of Egyptian life that during the first dynasty (3200 B.C.) a hieroglyph of a bee was the symbol of Lower Egypt, which became known as "Bee Land."

A worker bee collects pollen from tiny blossoms.

Honey was revered in Egypt, and figured prominently as both a foodstuff and in religious rites. As M. F. K. Fisher wrote in *Serve It Forth*, "Honey from the richly flowered delta had already in those far days been changed into a hundred kinds of sweetmeats, or baked into breads, or simmered with the flesh of melons and fruits to make the same heavy voluptuous confitures that travelers eat today in Alexandria." Because of its healing properties and abilities as a preservative, honey was regarded as a particularly powerful elixir, appropriate for feeding sacred animals and for making offerings to the gods. Corpses could be preserved in honey, while beeswax and honey were used in many cosmetic preparations. Records show that migratory beekeeping was widely practiced, as beekeepers moved their hives around to avoid flooding and follow the nectar flow as plants blossomed around the country.

During this period, references to honey crop up in written literature in China and India. The *Rig-Veda*, one of the most ancient Indian religious texts, refers repeatedly to the medicinal values of honey. But it was during the rise of the Greek and Roman empires that our most lasting guides to apiculture and honey were written.

Although he surmised erroneously that honey was "dew distilled from the stars and the rainbow," most of Aristotle's descriptions (344–342 B.C.) of the natural life of the honeybee remain remarkably accurate. Honey can be found throughout the *Iliad* and the *Odyssey*. In 401 B.C., Xenophon records a time when exhausted soldiers returning from one of Cyrus's expeditions gorged themselves on wild honey found near their camp. As Xenophon watched, his soldiers began staggering and vomiting, unable to control their legs and afflicted with violent nausea, diarrhea, and hallucinations. A similar distress afflicted a battalion of Pompey's troops. The cause was later discovered to be the honey, which the bees had made from nectar gathered from a certain species of rhododendron. (While poisonous honey is extremely rare, another soldier, this one from the American Civil War, reported a similar experience with honey made from the American mountain laurel.)

Roman authors were no less entranced by the intricacies of bee lore. Ovid's *Medicamina* mentions the use of honey and wax for medicinal as well as cosmetic purposes. An in-depth description of bees and beekeeping occupies most of Virgil's *Fourth Georgic*, including a graphic retelling of the Greek myth of Aristaeus, the god associated with beekeeping.

Pliny (A.D. 23–79) spends many pages of his *Natural History* on beekeeping and honey, agreeing with Aristotle that the best honey was gathered from bees foraging on wild thyme on the slopes of Mt. Hymettus in Greece, followed by that from Hybla on Mt. Etna in Sicily. Basing their theories on close observation, the Roman authors Columella and Varro remained the definitive authorities on the subject for much of the last two millennia, and can be read even now for useful information.

Where was all this honey going? For sweetening, of course, but not always in desserts. Ancient Roman and Greek cuisines balanced sweetness with tart, bitter, and savory flavors to a much wider degree than we do now, with less of an emphasis on dishes that are sweet from start to finish. Instead, honey, along with vinegar, was used as a flavoring with a vast number of herbs and spices. Thus embellished, honey and vinegar formed the basis for untold numbers of sauces, from dips for roast meat, fowl, and fish to light dressings for lettuces and salad greens. Other sauces were made from honey mixed with *garum* or *liquorum,* intensely salty liquids made from sun-rotted fish entrails, which were the most popular flavoring agents of the day, equivalent to the use of soy sauce in Chinese cooking or fish sauce in Thailand and Vietnam. Wine was rarely drunk straight; instead, it was mixed with water, sweetened with honey, and again flavored with herbs, spices, and plant resins. Honey was also used as a preservative, along with brine and vinegar, for meat, fruits, and vegetables.

In Scandinavian and Northern European countries too far north for grape cultivation, wine was made from honey, and in fact the bulk of the honey crop during the Middle Ages went to the making of this beverage, known as mead. Dozens of variations were developed, spiced and fermented in different ways, including metheglyn, hippocras, hydromel, bracket, pyment, and mulsum. Norse mythology even told how the great god Odin scorned all food in Valhalla, preferring to live on mead produced by Heidrun, his faithful goat. In England, Ireland, and Wales, mead consumption was widespread, as the many references to it in the epic poem *Beowulf* (A.D. 700) make clear. Meanwhile, in the Middle East and hence back to the Mediterranean, honey cultivation and use spread and thrived during the ascension of the Arabian empire between A.D. 600 and 800. Since alcohol was forbidden to Muslims, honey was predominantly used in food and medicine, as recommended by Mohammed in the Koran. This legacy, spreading through all of the Moorish-influenced cultures around North Africa, Sicily, Spain, and Turkey, is still seen in the predominance of honey-soaked and honey-sweetened pastries and confections in the cuisines of these cultures.

As the Catholic Church gained prominence in Europe, the need for beekeepers increased—not so much for the honey as for the beeswax that the bees produced. Clean burning, with a sweet scent and a clear flame, beeswax candles were much in demand for lighting churches during mass. But the aesthetic value of beeswax was not the only reason for its popularity. Produced as it was by "virgin bees," beeswax was seen as pure and particularly appropriate to Christian worship. Legend had it that the bees of Paradise fled when man sinned in Eden. For this demonstration of morality, the bees received God's blessing, and therefore "this blessing made it incumbent for candles made of their wax to be used whenever mass was sung." Apiculture became a skill cultivated by monasteries, with hives built in special bee gardens. St. Ambrose, bishop of Milan from 347 to 397, was established as the patron saint of beekeepers.

Meanwhile, in Jewish communities, honey had become an important component of festive occasions. Rosh Hashanah, the Jewish New Year, was celebrated with apples dipped in honey, symbolizing a wish for a sweet year to come. Round loaves of challah (a braided yeast bread enriched with eggs) were spread with honey, and the meal ended with slices of spiced honey cake and honey-sweetened fruit compotes. On the first day of a boy's enrollment in *chadar,* or religious school, letters from the Talmud would be written in honey on a slate and licked off by the new boys so as to make their learning sweet. Because of their industriousness in building up the combs of their hives, their connection with both Egyptian ritual and the Greek and Roman mystery cults, bees and beehives have long been a symbol for the Freemasons.

Myths and legends have always surrounded the practice of beekeeping. In rural Britain, the custom of "telling the bees" has persisted for centuries. Should any dramatic event—a wedding, a death—happen to a beekeeper's family, a member of the household must go out and share the information with the bees. Otherwise, legend has it, the bees will swarm away.

home sweet home

Imagine a beehive. What do you see? A skep, of course: woven of straw or wicker, shaped like a rounded cylinder, with a few bees buzzing around the top. From ceramic honey holders to the image on the state flag of Utah, this is the hive that persists in our collective memories, despite the fact that few, if any, people during the past century have ever seen an actual skep in use.

These days, an accurate mental picture of a beehive would involve something resembling a filing cabinet: a stack of wooden boxes, neat, simple, unromantic, and yet perfectly suited to the needs of both bees and beekeeper. But getting from hollow trees to skeps, and from skeps to modern hives, required centuries of research, development, and evolution.

As mentioned earlier, the first step in domesticating bees was to bring the bees to the beekeeper. Bee colonies naturally reproduce through swarming. When a hive gets too crowded, the workers raise a new queen. When that queen is ready to hatch, the old queen is forced out of the hive, along with about half the worker bees and a few drones. With their stomachs filled with honey, the bees depart en masse from the hive. After flying some distance, the swarm settles on a convenient tree limb or roof eave, the whole cluster forming a dangling, buzzing cone of bees. Then, scout bees are sent out to find a suitable new home—usually a hollow tree, a cave, or a cavity within a cliff.

With no home or honey to defend, bees in a swarm are actually more docile than bees in a hive. Thus, a resting swarm could be shaken intact into a basket or cloth bag (modern beekeepers have caught swarms using empty wooden hive boxes, cardboard boxes, or even pillow cases), since the swarm bees will cling together so as not to get separated from their queen. Sometimes, to avoid disturbing the bees, the whole tree branch on which the bees had settled would be cut off and the bees shaken into a a box. Once captured, the bees could be transported to a place of the beekeeper's choosing.

A well-protected beekeeper inspects a hive frame.

Once a swarm was caught, it needed a home, and like any other form of domestic architecture, hive structure varied and evolved from place to place. In Ethiopia, hives were made of mud and cow dung, while gourds, hollowed logs, and woven baskets were used elsewhere in Africa. In Egypt, bees were kept in mud-pipe hives; the bees entered from one end while the honey could be removed from the other. Later, mud was replaced with baked terra-cotta. In Greece, bees were kept in horizontal, wide-mouthed, thimble-shaped pottery hives. To make the honeycomb more accessible, some Greek beekeepers set their hives upright, with wooden bars set over the mouths of the hives so that the bees would build their comb directly down from the bars. Around the Mediterranean, thick strips of cork were shaped into upright, log-style hives, the round cork walls pinned together with wooden pegs. In the Middle East, cane and wicker hives were used.

All of these hives followed a roughly round or oval shape, to aid in the bees' formation of comb. Naturally occurring comb is always formed in an elongated oval shape, starting from the top of the hive and extending downwards. Bees will work on several sheets of comb at once, always building them at a set distance apart. This gap, usually between $\frac{3}{16}$ and $\frac{5}{16}$ of an inch, is known as "bee space." If a gap wider than this is left anywhere in the hive, the bees will instinctively fill it up, either with lumps of additional comb ("burr" comb) or with wads of propolis, also known as "bee glue." This sticky resin, collected from plant and tree sap, is worked by the bees into a quick-drying cement used to chink up every draft-attracting crack or crevice in the hive. Propolis also has antibacterial properties, which help prevent the growth of mold on the combs. While sealing up every gap inside the hive ensured a warm, cozy home for the bees, it was a habit that continued to frustrate their keepers. With all the honeycombs firmly attached to the inside of the hive, beekeepers couldn't collect honey without breaking into the hive and destroying it. Beekeepers struggled with this quandary for centuries; it was not until the mid-nineteenth century that the solution, based on the phenomenon of bee space, would be revealed, making possible the development of the modern movable-frame hive.

In medieval Germany, Hungary, and Poland, forest beekeeping—in which bee colonies were tended in living bee trees—remained the predominant means of honey production, although heavy, upright log hives were also used. Slowly, such clumsy wooden hives were replaced by skeps, light, movable hives of woven wicker or straw. Later, the predominant style of skep became a round-topped, conical hive made from tightly woven coils of straw. Easy to build from readily available natural materials, these skeps were usually spread over with cow dung or mud for weatherproofing (a process known as *clooming*), or covered with loose straw hackles to help the skep shed rain. As Eva Crane notes in *The Archaeology of Beekeeping*, "This kind of skep became the cult symbol of the bee colony, and also of industry, thrift, and the good attributes of a human community." Although the modern box hive replaced the skep over 150 years ago, the round, sturdy bulk of the skep still remains our primary image of a beehive.

Light, portable, easy to make, and fairly weatherproof, skeps could also be expanded. In the fifteenth and sixteenth centuries, coiled straw rings called ekes (as in "to eke out") were stacked under the skep. The comb would be harvested by sliding a wire between the eke and the skep, severing the comb within. The reverse could also be done, with straw caps placed on top of open-ended skeps.

While straw skeps had much to recommend them, harvesting the comb within usually required destroying the bees, most commonly by suspending the hive over a pit filled with sulfur fumes. Cutting the comb out was a messy business. And since a new swarm had to rebuild the combs from scratch after each harvest, much of the bees' energy was spent on comb building instead of honey production. The more energy the bees needed, the more honey they required for their own consumption, and the less honey would be left for the beekeeper at the end of the season. Beekeepers and naturalists continued to tinker with skeps, looking to improve the management of their hives and find a way to remove the combs without having to kill off the bees in order to harvest the honey.

The original Greek bar hives, with their suspended combs, had been a step in the right direction, although the combs hung down unevenly and couldn't be reused. By the middle of the eighteenth century, "carpenter's" hives were coming into common use. Instead of ekes beneath, these neat wooden-board hives were often built with wings on either side of the main hive. Brood was raised in the center, while surplus honey was stored in the sides, called supers. Smaller entrance holes into the side boxes prevented the queen from entering and laying eggs. In some wooden hives, the original skep caps were replaced with bell jars, which could be removed, comb and all, when filled. By the early nineteenth century, the modern hive as we know it was well on its way, with movable, framed combs, tiered boxes for honey storage,

Jars of wildflower honeys from different regions;
the opaque honey is creamed

and separate chambers for brood and honey; but the problem of *keeping* the combs movable remained. Left to their own devices, bees would solidly glue up every movable part of a hive with propolis, cementing the frames to the cover and sides of the hive. Francois Huber, a highly regarded Swiss naturalist and author of *Observations on the Honeybee* (1792), had invented a folding-leaf or "book" hive that greatly facilitated observation of the colonies within but was impractical for honey production.

Finally, the key to modern beekeeping was discovered by the Reverend L. L. Langstroth, a Philadelpia beekeeper and naturalist. The concept of bee space was already known, but Langstroth was the first to apply it to the challenge of creating a movable-frame hive. What Langstroth found was that if a bee space was left between the ends of the frame and the hive walls, as well as between the top of the frames and the inner cover, the bees would not need to fill in the excess spaces around the frames. Such a precisely measured hive would require no architectural adjustments in the shape of burr comb and propolis. Thus, the hive could be opened and the frames removed without breaking up the hive. In 1853, Langstroth published his findings in *The Hive and the Honeybee*, a text still used by beekeepers today.

Once the Langstroth hive came into common usage, additional developments followed quickly. In 1857, Johannes Mehring invented the foundation comb: ready-made sheets of honeycomb that mimicked the hexagonal pattern of wax cells produced by the bees themselves. With sheets of this foundation wired to the frames of his hive, the beekeeper could give his bees a jump-start on creating a usable comb. Rather than beginning from scratch, the bees could simply draw out the pattern of cells, extending each wall until the cell was deep enough to hold honey, pollen, or larvae. Shortly thereafter, the "queen excluder" came into use. This was a screen with holes wide enough to allow a worker bee through but too small for a queen. Placed between the main hive body and the stack of supers above, it assured the beekeeper that only honey, not brood, would be stored in the supers.

Honey processing was evolving, too. Honey was not always the clear, limpid liquid that is marketed today. For centuries, honey was stored or sold still sealed in the comb (what is known today as comb honey). Alternately, the comb was crushed and the honey drained out through a cloth bag. Even so strained, it was common to find wax, pollen, propolis, and bee debris floating in the honey. In 1865, the first centrifugal honey extractor was invented in Austria. Placed in a drum, the frames of honeycomb were whirled around at high speed, hurling the honey out of the cells without damaging the comb. Extracted honey was cleaner, and purer than strained honey, and the emptied comb could easily be returned to the hive. This is the way liquid honey is still proccessed today.

But while technology in the apiary was increasing, the world's everyday demand for honey was dropping. During the sixteenth century, the Reformation led to the dissolution of hundreds of monasteries across Europe. With the destruction of the monasteries went the beehives the monks had cultivated. The Church's great need for beeswax was ebbing at the same time that sugar was coming into Europe in ever-increasing quantities—and at ever-lowering prices. In Germany during the thirteenth century, sugar was a rare and expensive condiment, considered, on account of its scarcity, to be more of a spice or flavoring than a food. In contrast, honey, gathered for centuries from local forests, was a staple. But as opportunities for global trade slowly expanded in the centuries to follow, sugar became a commodity of ever-increasing prominence. Fortunes could be made in sugar and its important by-products, molasses and rum. As European colonization reached into the Tropics, sugarcane plantations followed. In Northern Europe, successful cultivation of the sugar beet lessened the need for honey. As the Industrial Revolution took hold, once-rural populations shifted from countryside to town; food was no longer consumed within a few miles of being raised. Unlike honeycomb, sugar was light, dry, and easy to transport—and increasingly affordable. From plantation to pastry shop, sugar became an international industry while honey stayed home.

Gradually, the symbolism of the bee shifted from product to process. From being famed for the sweetness of its honey—a taste associated with romance, innocence, and rural leisure—the bee now gained fame for the industriousness of its production methods. Prior to this, philosophers and politicians alike had looked to the hive as a model for a self-regulating society. Ever flexible, the beehive then became a symbol of the modern factory, with each bee working ceaselessly at a series of perfectly integrated tasks. In British heraldry during the nineteenth century, bees on a coat of arms often denoted achievement in industry—of titles earned, not inherited.

Out West, Mormon pioneers saw the beehive as the perfect symbol of their Utopian vision: a community in which the needs of every individual would be met by devotion to the colony as a whole. Mormon settlers originally dubbed Utah "the provisional state of Deseret," a name derived from the word for honeybee in the Book of Mormon. While the name Deseret was discarded in favor of Utah when the area became a United States territory in 1850, the state flag still bears a drawing of a beehive over the motto "Industry," and the honeybee remains the official state insect.

Although honey had been revered for centuries as a pure and natural product, the rise of cheap sugar and the invention of the extractor and new sweetening products such as corn syrup led to unscrupulous practices. Now that honey was no longer sold in the comb, what was to stop a corrupt producer from dosing up his honey with dissolved sugar, glucose, or corn syrup? Food adulteration had been a widespread problem for centuries (although it probably reached its nadir in eighteenth-century Britain, when alum, bone ash, and chalk often outweighed the actual grain in a loaf of bread), but in 1890, a sampling of five hundred types of American honey revealed that fully 37 percent were "grossly adulterated." These findings, sent to the government, assisted in the passage in 1906 of the Pure Food and Drug Act. Goaded by the government and pressured by ethical honey producers to push for scrupulous honesty in labeling, the honey industry squeezed out the corn-syrup adulterers and spurious "mock honey" makers.

While the country's demand for sugar has far outstripped its need for honey, honey has remained a friendly sight on supermarket shelf and breakfast table alike, sold clear and cheap in plastic honey bears topped with jaunty yellow caps or thick and topaz-cloudy in decorative skep-shaped jars. Just as jam making, cheese making, and bread baking have gone from something every farm wife could do to revered artisanal skills, so have small honey producers suddenly found room for their products on gourmet-store shelves, alongside the equally polished bottles of lovingly produced boutique vinegars and olive oils. But the best place to find honey may be right at the source. Many family-run honey operations keep their sales close to home, selling their products at farmers' markets or roadside stands. These are the honeys to treasure, made as a labor of love and ripe with the unmistakable flavors of the neighboring landscape. Every beekeeper has a story, and whether you discover eucalyptus honey in California, blueberry honey in Maine, or tupelo honey in Florida, buying a jar straight from the source lets you capture a taste of the fields and meadows, the mountains and forests warmed by the sun through the turning of the seasons.

chapter 2

one drop of nectar:

how honey is made

So work the honey-bees, creatures
that by a rule in nature teach
the act of order to a peopled kingdom.

William Shakespeare,
Henry V, *act 1, scene 1*

To make honey, first you need a flower, then you need a bee. The original source of honey is nectar, a sweet, sugary liquid offered up by many different types of flowers as a lure to hungry insects. Why would a flower want to seduce—or at least attract—a bug? For sex, of course, or more accurately, to promote cross-pollination.

Many plants contain both male and female reproductive organs in one flower. But to encourage reproductive diversity, most of these flowers have developed special protections against self-pollination. Sometimes, the anthers at the end of the flower's (male) stamen release their pollen spores before the (female) stigma is ready. By the time the stigma is receptive, the anthers may be withered, requiring a fresh infusion of pollen from another plant. Other plants produce separate male and female flowers, requiring a physical transfer of pollen from one to the other. Like Sleeping Beauty, the flowers lie waiting for the enlivening kiss of a pollinating insect, all the while wafting out an alluring scent of nectar.

Just as the flower is dependent on the bee, so is the bee dependent on the flower. All of the bee's food sources are concentrated in the flower: nectar, which is nearly pure carbohydrate, supplies energy to the working bee, while protein-rich pollen nourishes growing infant bees. Resins collected from the surfaces of certain plants are transformed into propolis, the sticky, malleable substance that the bees use to seal up every crack and crevice in the hive, rendering it warm and draft-free (no mean feat considering that optimal hive temperature is 95°F). For bees, honey is a remarkably efficient food source: on one ounce of honey, a bee could fly all the way around the world.

Since bees collect pollen as well as merely transporting it, flowers produce it extravagantly, pumping out thousands of grains per blossom. Successful flowers have also evolved with their nectaries (nectar-producing glands) tucked deep within their petals, so that wandering bees can't just sip and run. Instead, wiggling her long proboscis into the nectary, the bee bumps around the flower, finally emerging thickly powdered with pollen. So dusted, she will proceed to the next flower and the next, tracing a trail of pollen through the hundreds of flowers she visits in a day.

In the United States, honeybees accomplish an estimated 80 percent of crop insect pollination. Approximately 15 percent of our daily diet comes directly from insect-pollinated plants; another 20 percent from animals such as cows that forage off of insect-pollinated plants such as alfalfa and clover. It takes nearly a million honeybee colonies just to pollinate California's almond crop, which covers roughly 400,000 acres. In fact, with the current decimation of many wild bee colonies by the deadly varroa mite, as well as by pesticides and loss of habitat, farmers have become more dependent than ever on commercial beekeepers to ensure the pollination of their fruit trees and other crops. Farmers and beekeepers now have symbiotic relationships, much like those between the flowers and the bees themselves.

When a bee reaches a nectar-bearing plant, she sucks the tiny drop of sucrose, fructose, and water into her honey stomach, a special expandable receptacle separated from her own stomach by a valve. (Should she need food while flying, she can release this valve and shunt nectar into her actual stomach—a uniquely efficient system!) She can visit anywhere from fifty to a hundred plants before she needs to return to the hive and release her load. While foraging, the bee begins to secrete invertase, a digestive enzyme that breaks down the sucrose in the nectar into fructose and glucose, simpler sugars that can be more easily absorbed. When she reaches the hive, she is met by a younger hive bee who will beg the nectar off of her, accepting it into her own mouth. Relieved of her burden, the foraging bee will return to the field to seek new flowers. If she has found a particularly rich source of nectar, she will give directions to the other bees of the hive by means of a bee dance. Waggling and turning in the air, the bee uses a remarkable form of physical shorthand to indicate the distance, sensory landmarks, and angle of the sun in regard to a given location. The more vigorous the dance, the more enthusiasm is conveyed to the rest of the colony. Until the Austrian scientist Karl von Frisch's pioneering work recording and deciphering the bee dance in 1923 (published as *Aus dem Leben der Bienen* in 1927, later translated into English and published as *The Dancing Bees* in 1955), it was not known how bees were able to communicate the location of nectar sources so efficiently. As von Frisch discovered, round dances indicated a food source nearby; a waggle dance meant food was farther away, with the duration of the dance corresponding to the distance, and the direction determined by the bee's orientation toward the sun. (For this and other work in the field of insect communications and behavioral physiology, von Frisch was awarded a Nobel Prize in 1973.)

Back inside the hive, the hive bee is now squeezing the nectar from her mouth into her own honey stomach and back again, adding enzymes and, most importantly, exposing the nectar to air in order to evaporate out its excess water. In its original state, nectar is nearly 80 percent water. Were it to be stored this way in the hive, airborne yeasts would quickly feed off its sugars, fermenting and souring it (much as yeasts act on honey and water during the making of mead, or honey wine). In order to turn spoilage-prone nectar into thick, nearly inert honey, the percentage of water must be forced down to less than 20 percent. This is done first by the bees directly (as described above) and then by fanning the honey ripening in the comb. As the hexagonal cells of the combs fill up with drops of nectar, the bees inside the hive split into groups. Using their double sets of wings, which can flap 11,400 times a minute, one group fans fresh air into the hive, while the other fans damp, moisture-laden air out, the two groups acting as living dehumidifiers for the hive. This determined flapping is what causes the "buzz" of a hive, low and mild when the bees are busy and content, higher and louder when they are threatened or agitated. Experienced beekeepers can often judge the mood of a hive just from the noise it produces.

The high temperature of the hive—which is maintained by the metabolization of the bees themselves, and kept at a steady heat of 92° to 95°F—also encourages rapid evaporation. After a few days, the bees cap the fully ripened honey with a thin layer of beeswax. It will remain there until needed as food for the hive or until harvested by the beekeeper. In producing one pound of honey, a colony may fly more than fifty thousand miles back and forth from flower to hive. Even more stunning is the fact that over the course of her entire lifetime, a worker bee makes less than ¹⁄₁₂ of a *teaspoon* of honey.

Few animal communities are as regimented by sex and task as those of *Apis mellifera*. The average hive ranges from thirty to sixty thousand bees. Of these, the vast majority are sexually immature females, known as worker bees. They are well named, for the workers do virtually all the work of the hive, from building honeycomb and nursing the infant brood to foraging for nectar, water, and pollen and storing honey.

Above: A worker bee is drawn to a bounty of pollen offered by a poppy
Below: Rich, amber-colored honeycomb

Reproduction, however, is the sole province of the queen bee. All female bee larvae begin the same; whether a bee becomes a worker or a queen is dependent solely on the food she is given. Every fertilized bee larva is fed nutrient-rich royal jelly, which is made up of two fluids secreted from two glands in the head of the young larvae-tending nurse bees. After two days, every larva but that of the queen is changed to a diet of honey and pollen. Fed on royal jelly for a full six days, the queen grows much longer than her worker sisters. Most importantly, her rich diet triggers the full development of her reproductive organs. Of all the female bees in the colony, only a queen can mate and reproduce. Queens mate on the wing, leaving the hive for only one period of mating during their lifetimes. Once outside the hive, the queen attracts a crowd of male drones (born from unfertilized eggs) from surrounding colonies. The drones impregnate her one by one, and then, with their reproductive organs torn from their bodies by the vigor of their mating, fall to the ground and die. During her mating flight, the queen collects enough sperm to fertilize the hundreds of thousands of eggs she will lay in her lifetime. (If she does not collect enough sperm on her first flight, she may go back out over the course of several days on additional trips.) Laying eggs is the queen's sole task inside the hive. She lays seven days a week, twenty-four hours a day, producing anywhere from a thousand to fifteen hundred eggs in a single day.

Each egg, looking like a tiny grain of rice, is deposited into a single six-sided cell within the honeycomb. Concentric circles of brood are surrounded by larders of honey and pollen, also packed into six-sided cells. The mouth of each cell is tilted slightly upward, to make sure both eggs and honey stay snug within. After three days, the eggs hatch into grublike white larvae. Over the next six days, they are first fed royal jelly, then honey and pollen, after which they seal themselves into hard, brownish cocoons. Their cells are covered with a cap of beeswax for the next twelve days. Three weeks after the queen first laid the egg, a new bee chews her way out of her cell.

The first task of these newly hatched bees is to feed and tend the growing larvae. Only these young nurse bees produce the special enzymes needed to make up royal jelly, the body-building booster that helps the infant bee larvae triple in size during their first six days. Later, these nurse bees from the hive, become hive bees, tending and feeding the queen, removing debris and dead bees from the hive, and building fresh comb out of minute flakes of wax secreted by glands in their abdomens.

Their next step is out to the porch in front of the hive, guarding the entrance against predators or honey-thieving robber bees from other colonies. Finally, after approximately a month in the hive, the worker becomes a forager, gathering pollen and nectar from the surrounding plants to support the colony. Most nectar is collected from flowers blooming within a half-mile radius of the hive; while a worker can, and will, fly up to five miles to gather nectar, the ratio of energy consumption to production is most efficient when she is making short flights. Straying farther than a half a mile at a time also increases the chance of a bee getting caught by sudden weather or temperature changes.

The lifespan of a worker bee is most accurately measured in miles rather than days. Five hundred miles is about the limit a bee can fly in her lifetime. During the frenzy of honey flow—those months during the spring, summer, and early autumn, when the plants around the hive are in full nectar-laden bloom—most worker bees wear out their wings in a mere six weeks. By the time they've flown five hundred miles, their wings have been reduced to nothing but tattered stubs. As their reward, they are picked up by other, fitter bees and dropped away from the hive. Unable to fly back, removed from the warmth and community of the colony, they soon expire. In contrast, bees born at the end of summer, when the nectar flow is slowing down, may live until the following year, since they will spend most of their time inside the hive, clustered in a heat-conserving ball around the queen.

Drones, the couch potatoes of the colony, are well taken care of during the heady days of brood rearing and honey flow. Once the hive begins to settle down for the winter, with no more food coming in until spring, the workers start barring drones from the hive. Unable to feed themselves or subsist without the warmth of the hive, the drones quickly die. Drones still within the hive are attacked, stung, and driven out of the hive to die. The colony itself expands and contracts in size throughout the year. At the height of the nectar flow, the population may top fifty thousand bees, all of which are needed to tend the brood and produce enough honey to sustain the hive. Around the time of the autumn equinox, cued by the shortening hours of daylight, the queen slackens the pace of her egg laying. During the winter, the number of bees in the hive may drop down to ten thousand.

Even the queen is not exempt. Once the queen is established in the hive, the workers will go to any length to protect her. Indeed, the identity of the hive is dependent on

Here, the side entrance to this skep doubles as a pollen trap, scraping the dust off the bee's body upon entrance, making it easier for the beekeeper to collect bee pollen.

a pheromone that the queen spreads among the workers who tend to her. Diffused throughout the colony, this queen substance makes each bee in the colony instantly recognizable to the other bees in the hive. Bees attempting to enter the hive without this scent identifier are immediately pegged as robber bees intent on stealing the colony's supplies. (Unless, like party crashers bearing six-packs, they stumble in already bearing full loads of nectar. In this case, they are usually welcomed in and made part of the colony.) As beekeepers have learned, it is impossible to move a community of bees from one hive to another without securing the queen. Once the queen is moved, the rest of the bees will follow. If the queen has died or been killed, and the hive has not had time to raise a new one, the beekeeper can introduce a new queen into the hive. But put directly into an unfamiliar group of bees, the new queen would be quickly stung to death as an interloper; it must be done gradually. This is often accomplished by means of a small cage that lets the workers see and smell her while allowing her a protective royal distance. A small sugar food-plug is inserted in one end of the cage. The bees, busily eating their way through the sugar, eventually find their enmity subsumed by collective work and the pleasures of sugar (which is digested and stored in the comb cells much as nectar would be). By the time the plug is chewed through, the queen will be accepted.

Interestingly enough, the reproductive process of the honeybee was a mystery until fairly recently. Until the publication of Charles Butler's treatise, *The Female Monarchy* in 1609, the head of the hive was widely assumed to a male king bee. Those who had set great store by the purity of the industrious, hardworking honeybees were initially dismayed at the wantonness of the queen's nuptial flight, in which she mates on the wing with dozens of drones.

the honey harvest

Depending on the flowering cycles of their food sources, bees can make honey throughout the spring, summer, and early autumn. Once the honey has been ripened in the comb, it can be harvested at any time by the beekeeper.

In early spring, when winter honey stores have been depleted and few plants are blooming, the beekeeper must be careful to leave enough honey for the bees themselves, especially since this is also the time of intensive brood-rearing. Once the hive is strong and well-stocked with honey, the surplus honey can be taken off throughout the season to be replaced by empty frames of comb ready to be filled.

Bees are efficient creatures. Once they find a good source of nectar, they will alert their fellow workers as to its location, and all the bees of a hive will assiduously work the blossoms until every bit of the nectar is collected. Since blossoming of different plants occurs at various times of the year, an observant beekeeper knows when his or her bees are working the eucalyptus blossoms versus when they'll be deep in clover. Hence, the beekeeper can time the harvest with a particular nectar flow, thus assuring that most of the honey collected will actually be of one kind. Migratory beekeepers move their hives around (sometimes even to a different state) to follow the nectar flows or to assist local farmers with pollination.

A good colony can produce an excess (beyond what the hive needs for survival) of 30 to 50 pounds of honey per year. The United States has an annual honey yield of just over 200 million pounds. California is the leading state when it comes to honey production, with a yearly average of 30 million pounds, followed by North Dakota (27 million pounds), South Dakota (23 million pounds), Florida (23 million pounds), Texas (8 million pounds), Montana (7 million pounds), Michigan (6 million pounds), Wisconsin (6 million pounds), and Idaho (5 million pounds).

Imported honey has become increasingly important to commercial honey producers. Argentina, Mexico, Australia, and China all provide honey to American companies. Because honey is a seasonal product, large-scale honey processing plants usually rely on a mixture of domestic and imported honeys to ensure a steady supply of honey to their customers throughout the year.

from comb to bottle

A modern honey house can be a single warm, sweet-smelling room—or a tremendous, clattering factory ribboned with thousands of feet of pipes. No matter where, virtually all liquid honey is now produced by extraction.

To extract the honey, the frames of honeycomb must first be uncapped. Using various methods from an electric knife to an uncapping machine, the thin layer of beeswax sealing the cells is sliced off or broken. The open frames, now oozing honey, are arranged in a hollow cylindrical drum with a spout at the bottom. The drum is switched on and the frames begin whirling inside. Centrifugal force hurls the honey out of the combs. As it runs down the sides of the drum, it pours through the spout and is collected in a pipe or bucket for further filtration. At this point, the honey still contains pollen grains, bits of wax, and debris, including the occasional stray feeler or bee wing. It can be hand-strained through metal or cloth filters, which catch larger bits of debris while allowing some pollen grains to go through, or mechanically filtered using heat and pressure to remove foreign materials. Because filtration takes out even the smallest bit of material around which a crystal could form, filtered honey is more likely to stay clear and liquid for a long time. At this stage, honey can also be pasteurized. Unlike milk or fruit juice, honey is already a very unfriendly medium for bacterial growth; heat is used to safeguard against yeast spores, which can cause fermentation over time, especially in honeys with a high water content.

is raw honey better?

Many honeys, especially those found in natural-food stores, are labeled "raw" or "uncooked" honey. As anyone who's ever tried to scrape a spoon through a jar of cold honey knows, honey has to be kept warm during the bottling process.

In the hive, the honey is naturally kept at a temperature between 92° and 95°F—just a few degrees under human body temperature. Many beekeepers agree that honey can be heated between 112° and 120°F without any significant change in flavor, aroma, or texture. This is warm enough to keep the honey moving but not so hot as to cook it, especially if the honey is bottled promptly. Heating the honey beyond 120°F can destroy some of its trace vitamins as well as destroying some of the volatile elements of taste and aroma.

Heating, filtering, and blending honey produces a clear, sparkling, reliable product that is unlikely to crystallize. Since the amount of vitamins and minerals found in honey is extremely small, many honey producers and nutritionists feel that there is little, if any, nutritional difference between raw and processed honeys. However, heat can destroy enzymes and certain volatile taste components, so if you are interested in exploring the homeopathic values of honey, or are just interested in tasting the true flavors of a particular kind of honey, it's worth it to seek out sources for raw honey. As a rule, raw honey is usually minimally processed, strained by hand through cheesecloth or metal sieves and hand-bottled. As a result, the honey retains more individual characteristics, with more complex flavors than those found in regular commercial honeys.

From buttery yellow to rich mahogany, wildflower honeys
are as distinct in color as they are in flavor.

medicinal uses of honey

Honey has long been touted as an all-purpose panacea, able to soothe sore throats, nourish convalescents, prevent infections, and give instant energy. In the days before widespread refrigeration, honey's antibacterial properties made it indispensable as both a preservative and an infection fighter.

Different honeys have various levels of antibacterial agents; some are reputed to be effective against virulent bacteria such as staphylococcus. With its high density and acidity, honey presents a very unfriendly medium for bacterial growth. Hydrogen peroxide, occurs naturally in low concentrations in honey, further contributing to its purifying abilities. Honey mixed with vinegar or lemon juice in tea or hot water has often been used as a home remedy for sore throats. Dressing a wound or burn with honey can promote healing, fight infection, and help prevent scarring by keeping the skin moist and preventing bandages from sticking to raw skin. Propolis, a sticky substance made by bees from tree sap and resin, is also naturally high in antibacterial properties. Propolis tinctures have a long history of use in Europe as a folk remedy.

Historically, the usefulness of honey continued even after death. In the ancient world, a general killed in battle far from home would be submerged in a coffin filled with honey. Sealed, the coffin could then be transported back for burial without fear of putrefaction along the way. Supposedly, Alexander the Great was buried in a gold coffin filled with the purest white honey. In England in the sixteenth and seventeenth centuries, a certain aristocratic family revived this tradition by burying each newly deceased earl in a lead coffin filled with honey. On a similar note, the ancient Romans used honey (along with brine, pitch, and oil) to preserve the heads of traitors, criminals, and enemies of the state who had been killed outside Rome. The heads, thus preserved for identification, were brought back to Rome and put on public display in the Forum.

The potency of honey as an antibacterial agent is significantly decreased by heat. Therefore, honey used for topical purposes should always be raw, minimally processed honey. Naturally, severe burns, cuts, and abrasions should always be treated by a trained medical professional. But minor burns or shallow cuts can be soothed with a dab of honey.

homeopathic honey

Hay fever sufferers who greet the arrival of spring with runny noses and streaming eyes may find relief in honey. If you're lucky, as little as a tablespoon a day can ease the symptoms of pollen-related allergies. But not just any honey. In order to desensitize this overactive immune response, the honey should come from a local source of the same flowers causing the allergy. Traces of pollen in the honey may then have a homeopathic effect, decreasing the impact of airborne pollen. To be most effective, homeopathic honey should be harvested within a fifty-mile radius of where you live.

Honey is not the only medical medium produced by bees. Beekeepers have long sworn by the efficacy of bee stings in treating arthritis. As a result, many alternative-medicine practitioners have begun using injections of bee venom to ease the pain and cramping of arthritis in the hands and joints. (Of course, this form of treatment should never be used on a patient with a severe bee sting allergy.)

instant energy

Honey is a dense, calorie-packed food—about sixty-four calories per tablespoon. For athletes in need of a last-minute burst of instant muscle fuel, this is great news. Even better is the fact that invertase, a digestive enzyme secreted in the bee's honey stomach, has already broken down the sucrose in the nectar into fructose and dextrose (also known as glucose), two monosaccharides, or simple sugars, that can be instantly absorbed into the bloodstream. (Interestingly enough, invertase is the same enzyme produced by the human pancreas to break down sucrose—the "sugar" of table sugar—into usable glucose.) To get this honey boost, try adding a spoonful of honey to your water bottle when biking, running, or working out. Keep drinking after your workout, too, as honey can help muscles recuperate and restore glycogen levels. Honey also includes antioxidants as well as trace amounts of numerous vitamins and minerals, including potassium, niacin, thiamin, riboflavin, and pantothenic acid.

Bee pollen is an excellent source of energy and a great addition to smoothies

In addition, many alternative medical practitioners view royal jelly, the food bees feed larvae, as an immune booster and energy food. Bee pollen, collected from the hive and pressed into small granules, is a great source of protein. Both royal jelly and bee pollen can be used as dietary supplements.

babies
and
honey

If you're a new parent, you may have been told never to feed honey to your baby. That's right! **Children under twelve months of age should not eat honey in any form.** On very rare occasions, honey can harbor certain bacterial spores that can cause infant botulism. While the chance of finding these spores in a jar of honey is very slim, infant botulism is a serious disease that affects the nervous system. Once a child is over a year old, his or her digestive system will have developed enough to handle any such spores without incident. Honey poses no health threat to adults, or children over twelve months of age.

chapter 3

backyard
beekeeping

She found me roots of relish sweet,
And honey wild, and manna dew,
And sure in language strange she said—
"I love thee true."

John Keats,
"La Belle Dame sans Merci"

Getting started with bees is less like gardening and more like starting up a miniature livestock operation in your backyard. But just as you can make even an urban backyard into a flourishing oasis, bees can thrive nearly anywhere with the proper care and attention.

As gardening enriches both the soil and the landscape, so bees enrich the agriculture around them through pollination. More pollination, of course, means more fruits and vegetables for everyone. Keeping bees is also good for the environment; with the varroa mite epidemic rapidly destroying native wild bees, raising the domestic bee population is more important than ever to ensure natural pollination of wild as well as cultivated plants.

Good for the environment, good for your garden . . . and then there's the honey. A single healthy hive can produce anywhere from ten to thirty pounds of surplus honey a year. So how do you get started? While you won't need to take your bees out for a walk or herd them into the barn at night, tending bees does require some specialized equipment and information. (The instructions laid out in the following pages are meant only as a general introduction; if you are seriously interested in keeping bees, refer to the Resources guide to find a list of books written specifically for the beginning beekeeper.) As with any other hobby, finding a place to get your questions answered is the most important first step. Here are a few tips:

go to the library
Books are a great place to start; you'll find a list of good introductory texts in the Resources section in the back of this book.

join a beekeeping club
Of the roughly 200,000 beekeepers in the United States, over 95 percent are non-commercial, hobbyist beekeepers, most with fewer than 25 hives. Local beekeeping organizations can be found across the country. Check with a university cooperative extension or horticultural society in your area. Besides being a place to meet and discuss ideas with other local beekeepers, beekeeping clubs often sponsor classes, lectures, and outings as well as providing access to shared equipment.

take a class
Many horticultural societies offer periodic classes or workshops in beekeeping. You can also try the local cooperative extension.

find a mentor
Beekeepers, as a rule, like to share their knowledge. If you're curious, and eager to learn, you're likely to find a more experienced beekeeper willing to take you around his or her hives.

research local beekeeping ordinances
Some communities forbid beekeeping; others have limits on the number of hives that can be kept in one place.

don't go overboard at the beginning
Start with two hives, not ten. Taking on too many bees at the start can lead to burnout and neglect, which won't benefit you or your hives.

don't go gadget-crazy
Start with the basics, and do a lot of asking around before you invest in any new "miracle" equipment.

don't cut off your learning curve
Bees are complex living creatures, and research into their lives and habits is constantly evolving. You can always keep learning.

don't be too scared to open your hives
Respect is healthy; after all, bee stings hurt! Start out slowly and learn how to behave around your bees. Once you know how and when to approach your bees, your confidence should increase.

don't assume you can make a living by selling your honey
There's a big gap between enjoying your bees as a hobby and actually turning a profit. Like any kind of farming, beekeeping is a very unpredictable endeavor. At least for the first year or two, just have fun, and look at the honey you end up with as a sweet side benefit, not as a means of quitting your day job.

making a home for your bees

Bees, like flowers, have two primary needs: sunshine and water. Bees need to keep their hive at a steady 92° to 95°F inside to ensure proper incubation of their brood. Setting up your hive in the right spot will help greatly in keeping the hive healthy and productive.

In most climates, bees prefer a hive in a sunny spot. If, however, you live in a very hot area, you may want to place your hive under a shady tree, where it can get morning or evening sun but will be protected from direct rays during the midday heat. Bees also need water, both to drink and for cooling the hive during hot weather. Any flat, shallow container (such as the top of a birdbath) will do, as long as you are diligent about keeping it filled with clean water at all times, especially during the summer. Make sure to scatter some small rocks through the water so the bees will have a place to stand as they drink.

Bees hate being cold and they don't like to be pushed around, so needless to say, wind is right at the top of their list of things to avoid. If you live in a particularly windy area, try to find a protected lee corner in which to set up your hive, or consider adding trees or bushes to form a windbreak around the hive. Face the entrance of the hive to the east or south to maximize warmth.

Bees are not the only ones who find a hive safe and snug. Ants, mice, skunks, and raccoons all find beehives irresistible. Positioning your hive at least one foot off the ground via concrete or wooden blocks surrounded by "moats" of diatomaceous earth may help keep out strolling ants and other critters. When setting up your hive, make sure to tip the entrance side slightly forward so that rainwater will not collect in the back of the hive and encourage rot and decay.

For safety's sake, place your hives in an inconspicuous spot in your yard or garden, well away from the reach of curious children, nervous neighbors, or romping dogs. If you live in a heavily trafficked area, especially one near a school or playground, you may want to ask a neighbor in a quieter, more secluded area to host your bees. It's a good idea to let your neighbors know that there are bees in your yard. Pointing out the difference between mild-tempered, hardworking honeybees (generally, only the few dozen guard bees at the entrance to the hive are disposed to sting) and aggressive, picnic-dogging yellow jackets or wasps, describing the environment's need for domestic pollinators due to the decline of wild native bees, and promising a few jars of honey every season can go far in soothing any misgivings.

why weeds are better than lawns

Few people would think of a city backyard as an ideal home for bees. However, many urban environments offer diverse, bee-friendly mixes of flowering trees, backyard vegetable patches, parks, and vacant-lot weeds, all of which can contribute to wonderful honey. Perfect, close-cropped suburban lawns, by contrast, are a desert for bees. What bees need are flowers, and as Emily Dickinson noted, "A clover, any time to him is Aristocracy." From blackberry vines to goldenrod to wild asters, bees are happy to sup on the kinds of scrubby wild plants that even gardeners rarely notice. While your garden will only provide a small portion of your bees' nectar, keeping it wild for the bees can be a great reason to loosen up your garden maintenance. Mild, temperate-to-warm climates that can support flowering plants year-round are, naturally, the best suited for beekeeping. Bees, however, are persistent, resourceful, and willing to fly up to five miles away to get nectar. As long as something's blooming in your vicinity from mid-spring through mid-autumn, your bees will find it.

building your hive

The standard and most economical way to buy a hive is to buy it "knocked down." This means you'll get it ready-cut but in pieces, with instructions for putting it together. Fully constructed hives are available, but are much more expensive. Make sure you allow plenty of time to build your hives before your bees arrive.

The parts of the hive (starting from the bottom up) are as follows:

hive stand
Wooden pallets, concrete blocks, scrap wood: anything to keep the hive off the ground to prevent dampness and keep pests away from the hive

bottom board
A wooden board that serves as the base of the hive

hive body
Also known as the brood chamber. The center of the hive, in which the bees will lay eggs, rear brood, and store honey and pollen. Usually comprised of one or two full-sized wooden boxes, also known as deep supers, holding ten frames of comb each.

frames
Removable wooden frames used for holding sheets of honeycomb. An average hive body or honey super holds ten frames.

foundation comb
Sheets of beeswax or plastic imprinted with hexagonal cell shapes and wired into the frames. Using foundation comb encourages neat, even, well-filled comb. Builds a more efficient hive, since bees have only to draw out the comb into deeper cells rather than building the comb from scratch.

A smoker sits next to an open hive ready to lull the bees,
making it easier for the beekeeper to collect the honeycomb

queen excluder
A metal or plastic screen large enough for workers to pass through, but too small for the queen. Placed between the hive body and the honey supers to keep the queen from laying eggs in the honey supers.

honey supers
Wooden boxes, either full-sized (deep) or half-sized (shallow), filled with frames of foundation comb. Honey is harvested from these honey supers only, to avoid disturbing the brood comb. Depending on the strength of the nectar flow, additional honey supers can be added throughout the season to give the bees more storage room. Remember, honey is twice as dense as water. A full deep super can weigh over fifty pounds, so many beekeepers prefer to use several shallow supers, which can be lifted more easily.

cover
Choices are a migratory (flat) cover or a telescoping (two-piece) cover.

You'll also need some additional materials, both for assembling your hive and for maintaining and protecting yourself and your hive:

latex paint
Hives should be painted to increase durability and weather resistance. Any good-quality exterior latex paint will work.

galvanized nails
For putting together your hive. Seven-penny nails are the best size for putting together hive bodies and supers. For the frames, order frame nails from a beekeeping supply source, as they are an unusual size.

hive tool
This flat, angled piece of metal is the beekeeper's best friend. Primarily used for prying frames out of the hive body, but indispensable for any number of jobs. Buy two, because you can't work on your hive without one.

smoker
A metal can with a bellows attached, used for blowing smoke into a hive to distract the bees before opening. Look for one with a guard around the outside.

bee brush
A soft, wide brush for brushing bees off the hive and frames. A soft, wide, clean paintbrush can also be used.

frame grips
Metal grips that aid in lifting frames from the hive. Not strictly necessary, but helpful, especially if you're wearing gloves.

spray bottles
One of water (for honey cleanup), one of alcohol, to cut through propolis

bee suit
A thick head-to-toe garment that covers the wearer securely and protects from stings

veil
Mesh protection for the head, neck, face, and ears. Folding veils are worn over wide-brimmed hats, while hatless veils, which resemble fencing masks, cover the head and face. Both veils come with strings that are tied crosswise across the chest to prevent bees from crawling inside.

gloves
Elbow-length gauntlet gloves, used to protect the beekeeper's hands and forearms. Thicker gloves offer more protection; however, they can be clumsy to use.

light-colored apron or coveralls
Beekeeping is a messy business. Propolis, or "bee glue," will mark whatever it touches. A heavy apron or pair of coveralls can save your clothes from getting permanently stained. Dark or bright colors tend to agitate bees, so wear light colors like white or beige if possible.

**using
used
hives**

Many of the beekeepers we spoke with warned against buying used hives. Hygiene is the main issue: since American foulbrood (AFB), one of the most serious of bee diseases, is spread through spores, it's often impossible to know if a hive has held diseased bees in the past. AFB can quickly decimate a colony, and while preventive measures can be taken, the only sure way to keep it from spreading once it has deeply infected a colony is to burn the hive (and its contents). Don't be tempted; always start with new, clean hive bodies and supers.

buying bees

It's springtime, the flowers are beginning to bud, and your hives are ready and waiting. Now, you need your bees.

Believe it or not, bees are sold by the pound and are delivered through the mail just like a sweater or a box of cookies. Well, not exactly like a sweater; instead of being packed in an envelope, the live worker bees are placed in a small box screened with fine wire mesh, with a can of sugar syrup to feed on during the journey. A queen is usually included in the colony; since she is often bred separately, a tiny protective queen cage is set up within the box, to keep the rest of the bees from attacking her as a foreign queen. Although the bees cannot get out of the cage, be prepared for your delivery to cause some agitation at the post office. Make sure a contact number is included in your order and be ready to pick up your bees as soon as they arrive. Once you pick them up, be sure to let them settle down overnight in a cool, dark spot before releasing them into the hive.

As you will quickly realize, a colony is a living organism, with a collective life cycle and personality all its own. Different colonies will develop different personalities and styles, about which you can learn every time you observe your hives. Setting up your hives is just the beginning; an association with bees can become a lifelong connection.

bee
stings

No matter how careful you are around your bees, getting stung is part of being a beekeeper. Wearing light-colored protective clothing (including a long-sleeved shirt with a collar you can tuck up under your veil, and long pants), using a smoker, keeping your movements slow and gentle, and not disturbing the hive during cold, wet, or windy weather can go far in preventing stings. You should avoid wearing strong scents (including perfume, lotions, certain cosmetics, and hair products) and dark or bright-colored clothing, all of which can agitate your bees.

While painful, bee stings rarely cause more than mild discomfort, mostly in the form of tenderness and swelling that begins shortly after being stung and subsides over the next twenty-four hours. Getting the stinger out as quickly as possible helps reduce the amount of venom absorbed, as a nerve ending attached to the stinger continues to pulse the venom under the skin even after the bee has dropped off. To remove a stinger, scrape (don't pinch or squeeze) the stinger out of the skin using gentle horizontal motions. Apply ice to the affected area. Over-the-counter topical medicines and oral antihistamines can help relieve itching. Some people can experience nonfatal but serious systemic reactions, involving hives and general swelling and itching around the face, hands, and feet along with nausea, fainting, or vomiting, especially if multiple stings occur at the same time.

The good news about stings is that during the first year, most beekeepers build up a basic immunity to bee venom, which greatly reduces the reaction. However, a very small number of people are fatally allergic to bee venom. In such cases, a single sting can send the victim into anaphylactic shock, in which rapid swelling closes the windpipe, leading to death. **Always consult your physician to have your susceptibility assessed before getting started with bees.** Many beekeepers keep an Epi-Pen (a sterile needle containing a dose of epinephrine, which can reverse the effects of anaphylactic shock) among the equipment they take out to the hive. Epi-Pens are available by prescription only; if you decide to add one to your kit, make sure you know exactly how and when to use it.

chapter *4*

* * *

from acacia
to wildflower:
the flavors of honey

Thy lips, O my bride, drip as the honeycomb:
honey and milk are under thy tongue . . .

Song of Songs

The flavor of any honey is wholly dependent on the bees' source of nectar. When one particular type of flower is in blossom, the bees will work it until all possible nectar is collected before moving on to the next type of bloom. Beekeepers often follow the blooms, moving their hives around so their bees will be within working distance of an area rich in a particular source.

While many factors can affect the final result, from weather and climate conditions to the type of processing used to finish the honey, the type of flower is the top element to consider when choosing a honey. As a result, most American and European honeys are labeled with the name of the tree or plant from which the nectar was harvested. In certain areas, such as in Greece, the location—what winemakers would call the *terroir*—can be found on the label along with the type of bloom.

Commercial, large-scale honey producers often blend their honeys to achieve a uniform result throughout the year. Thus, a jar of clover honey may be made up of honey harvested during several different clover nectar flows. Smaller scale, artisanal honey producers, who don't often have the facilities to store large quantities of honey, are more likely to bottle and sell their harvests throughout the year as each different honey ripens. At Marshall's Farm in California's Napa Valley, for example, one of the delights of autumn is their limited-quantity pumpkin blossom honey, produced by bees that have foraged in the pumpkin patch. One year, the honey may taste like pumpkin pie: spicy, creamy, and rich. The next year, the spiciness might be much less pronounced, with a mellow sweetness at the fore instead. Just as the weather is never exactly the same from one day to the next, so no honey is ever exactly alike from year to year.

Bees around the world visit thousands of different flowering plants to gather nectar; it would be a formidable task to list every type of honey. However, this list should help you identify familiar honeys as well as learn about some about lesser-known types.

If you've never tasted an unblended, varietal honey, ask to sample a few the next time you come upon a local honey producer at a roadside stand or farmers' market. Just as with different types of wine, the variations can be amazing. Far from simply sweet, fresh raw honey can be a continual surprise: one kind buttery and nut-like, another intensely perfumed and flowery. Keep tasting and trying until you find a honey you love.

acacia

This thorny, subtropical shrub blooms at around the same time as eucalyptus, providing a delicate, pale yellow honey.

alfalfa

A mild, pale golden honey produced from the blossoms of a grassy legume grown for animal fodder, found throughout the Midwest and Western states. Along with clover and orange blossom, one of the most popular types of American honey.

arbuta

Also known as *corbezzolo* or strawberry tree, this tree grows wild along the coasts of southern Italy and Sardinia; its red fruits are used for jam. The cloudy tan honey produced from its blossoms has a strong bitter aftertaste.

basswood

Also known as linden or lime tree. Nectar from these trees makes a favorite country honey, very pale with a lively, biting tang.

berry

The blossoming of blueberries, blackberries, and raspberries produces mild, fruity honeys, commonly found in New England, Michigan, and the Pacific Northwest.

buckwheat

Dark, brawny, and slightly bitter, this honey is harder to find now that buckwheat cultivation has declined and tastes have swung over to milder, lighter honeys. Good for cooking—use as a replacement for molasses in gingerbreads and spice cakes, or use like maple syrup over pancakes or waffles.

chestnut

During the last century, a chestnut blight caused by an imported fungus wiped out almost every indigenous American chestnut tree. Restoration projects (involving crossbreeding with blight-resistant Chinese chestnuts) have begun, but so far no American chestnut honey is available. However, dark, richly flavored chestnut honey from Italy is regarded as among the world's best honeys.

clover

Sunny, sweet, and light, this is a widely available, crowd-pleasing, and uncomplicated honey.

eucalyptus

One of the earliest bloomers, this Australian import, now common throughout California, provides a late-winter boost for Californian bees. Eucalyptus honey is pale yellow with a light green tinge and has a slightly herbal edge.

fireweed

Found growing wild throughout the Pacific Northwest, fireweed is a favorite of bees in Oregon and Washington. Fireweed honey is a light greenish-yellow with a mild, grassy-sweet flavor.

heather

This dark, full-flavored honey, a specialty of Scotland, is known for its remarkable jelly-like consistency.

kiawe

These Hawaiian trees produce an opaque, pearly white spreadable honey with a very mild, sweet flavor.

lavender

Flowery and very sweet, this honey has a distinct lavender scent and taste.

leatherwood

Harvested from the blossoms of the Tasmanian leatherwood tree, leatherwood honey has a spicy aroma and a complex, full-bodied flavor.

Apple blossoms, lavender flowers, and assorted wildflowers
offer a sweet bounty of nectar for spring's busy bees.

mangrove

Buttery, brown-sugar notes stand out in this tropical Southern honey.

manuka

This deep amber New Zealand honey is famed for its antibacterial properties.

manzanita

A dark, molasses-like honey from flowering native trees found mainly in California.

mesquite

Pungent and full-flavored, this Southwestern honey is good in savory dishes, especially barbecue sauces.

oak

A buttery, caramel-tasting dark honey.

orange blossom

Citrusy, fragrant, light amber in color, as are the other citrus honeys such as lemon blossom.

palmetto (or saw palmetto)

This Florida honey is strong, not too sweet, and deep orange-gold in color.

pumpkin

This deep amber honey has a sweet-spicy flavor reminiscent of pumpkin pie.

sage

Pale gold in color, sage honeys can vary in flavor, but tend to be mildly herbal.

sourwood

Common to the southern Appalachian Mountains, this Southeastern honey is pale with a fine mild flavor.

star thistle

Found in California and the Pacific Northwest, this pale greenish-gold honey has a pleasant, slightly grassy flavor.

sunflower

Popular in Germany, this pale amber honey is faintly tangy.

thyme

Highly prized along the Mediterranean, this dark honey has a distinct herbal/grassy flavor.

tupelo

This specialty honey never crystallizes. It is produced from the nectar of the tupelo gum tree, which grows along the Apalachicola, Choctahatchee, and Ochlockonee rivers and their tributaries in northwest Florida.

wildflower

A catchall term for honeys made from the nectar of a wide variety of flowers. They vary with the flower mix and location, but tend to be pleasantly floral and sweet.

cooking
with honey

The only reason for being a bee
that I know of is making honey . . .
and the only reason for making honey
is so I can eat it.

A. A. Milne,
Winnie-the-Pooh

A frothy smoothie, a slice of soft, spicy honey cake, a brimming bowlful of golden granola: no matter what you're in the mood for, honey is a natural in the kitchen. Keep a squeezable container of honey on your kitchen counter, and you're bound to find dozens of uses for it every time you start cooking.

Quick-dissolving honey makes a great sweetener for both hot and cold beverages—you'll find several to get you started here, from a refreshing ginger-honey soda to a vitamin C–packed hot honey lemonade. And if you need a last-minute fix on a dish, don't call the pizza guy—just grab your honey bear! If your tomato sauce is too tart, a teaspoon or two of honey can smooth out that acidic bite, while adding a few tablespoons of honey to the cooking water gives corn on the cob a farm-fresh sweetness.

With its mellow essence and gentle perfume, honey really shines in fruit desserts, baked goods, and extra-special condiments. And since a special jar of honey makes a wonderful gift, you'll find plenty of delicious go-along recipes. Bring a batch of Buzzing Bran Muffins to brunch, take a jar of Venetian Spiced Honey Preserves as a weekend hostess gift, or box up a batch of irresistibly crunchy baklava. You'll find that honey makes any baked item stay moist and fresh longer.

Honey can be easily substituted for corn syrup or molasses in most recipes by equal measure. When substituting honey for sugar in baking, start out by substituting honey for half the sugar originally called for. (If a recipe calls for 1 cup sugar, use ½ cup sugar and ½ cup honey.) Then, reduce the liquid called for in any recipe by ¼ cup for each cup of honey used. To counteract honey's natural acidity when baking, add ¼ teaspoon of baking soda for each cup of honey used. For easy measuring and cleanup, measure oil first, then honey, using the same cup.

Or, grease your measuring cup lightly with oil or cooking spray, and the honey will slip right out. One cup of honey equals one 12-ounce jar. Honey speeds up the baking process, so reduce the oven temperature by 25°F to prevent overbrowning.

Like sugar, honey can break down gluten, the protein necessary to hold bread dough together. Don't use more than ¼ cup honey per 2 cups of flour, and use high-protein or bread flour for best results. When heating honey, always use low heat and a large pot. It will bubble and foam up dramatically as it heats, so make sure to keep a close eye on the honey to prevent it from overflowing.

Honey should be stored in a closed container at room temperature. Although honey can last for many years, the flavor will be most vivid if consumed within a year of purchase. Left to itself, all honey will eventually crystallize, transforming from a thick, translucent or transparent liquid to a cloudy, solid mass as a result of the glucose naturally precipitating out into small, grainy crystals. Some honeys crystallize almost immediately; others may remain liquid for many months. Raw, unfiltered honeys are more prone to crystallization than honeys that have been heated and filtered. If crystallization occurs, don't worry! Your honey hasn't spoiled or gone bad; it has simply changed its molecular structure. You can reverse this by gently warming the jar in a pan of warm water until it returns to a liquid state, or by microwaving it on high for a few seconds at a time until liquified. Honey crystallizes much faster at temperatures below 57°F. Therefore, to keep your honey clear and free-flowing, store it in your pantry, NOT in the refrigerator.

※ ※ ※ ※ ※

honey power granola

Chock-full of fiber-rich whole grains, seeds, and dried fruits, this granola has just enough honey sweetness to make it perfect at any hour, whether you're fueling up in the morning, grabbing a quick snack, or unwinding over a one-bowl supper. Plus, it's incredibly easy to make—just mix, bake, and go!

2	cups old-fashioned rolled oats (not quick-cooking or steel-cut)
¾	cup sliced or slivered almonds
¼	teaspoon salt
¼	cup wheat bran (optional)
½	cup hulled sunflower or pumpkin seeds (optional)
½	cup canola oil (or any other mild-flavored vegetable oil)
½	cup honey
1¼	cups raisins
2	tablespoons bee pollen (optional)

Preheat oven to 325°F. Stir oats, almonds, salt, and wheat bran and sunflower or pumpkin seeds, if using, together in a large bowl. Add oil and honey, and stir until oat mixture is thoroughly moistened. Spread oat mixture on a large baking sheet and bake, stirring occasionally, until toasty and golden brown, 30 to 40 minutes. Remove baking sheet from the oven. Pour granola into a large bowl and stir in raisins and bee pollen, if using. Let cool completely. Store in airtight containers.

{ **yield:** approximately 6 cups }

continued ●▶

fruit basket granola

Substitute one or more of the following for the raisins: slivered dried apricots, dried cranberries, minced dates, dried cherries. Add 1 teaspoon grated orange or tangerine zest after baking.

autumn orchard granola

Add ½ teaspoon cinnamon and ¼ teaspoon ground nutmeg to the oat mixture before baking. After baking, add 1 cup slivered dried apples.

tropical delight granola

Add 1 cup shredded, dried coconut to the oat mixture before baking. After baking, substitute 1 cup minced dried papaya or mango and ½ cup crushed banana chips for the raisins.

* * * * *

buzzing bran muffins

Frankly, before developing this recipe, I'd given up on finding a healthy bran muffin that tasted good. Either they were clunky, dry, and too full of what one fiber-wary friend dubbed "sticks and leaves," or (the opposite approach) they were greased up with so much oil that I might as well have been eating a boxful of Krispy Kremes. These muffins, however, get their moistness from two great ingredients—honey and buttermilk—which keeps the added fat to a minimum. Even notoriously picky toddlers love these, especially when they're made "kid size" in a mini-muffin pan.

1	cup boiling water
1	cup wheat bran
¼	cup dark, full-flavored honey
4	tablespoons canola oil
1	cup raisins
1½	cups whole-wheat flour
1½	teaspoons baking soda
½	teaspoon salt
½	cup wheat germ
2	eggs, beaten
1	cup buttermilk

Preheat oven to 350°F. Grease a 12-cup muffin pan. In a large bowl, mix boiling water, bran, honey, oil, and raisins. Set aside for 5 minutes. Meanwhile, in another bowl, sift or whisk together flour, baking soda, salt, and wheat germ. Beat eggs and buttermilk together in a third bowl. Stir flour mixture into bran mixture. Add buttermilk mixture. Stir together lightly (do not beat). Fill muffin cups approximately ⅔ full. Bake 25 minutes, or until muffins spring back lightly when pressed with a fingertip. Let cool in pan for 10 minutes, then remove muffins to a rack to cool.

{ **yield:** 12 muffins }

* * * * *

honey~glazed challah knots

A round, raisin-studded challah bread is the centerpiece of every table on Rosh Hashanah, the Jewish New Year. Extra honey goes into the bread to ensure "a sweet year," then the bread is traditionally served with apples and more honey for dipping. While this bread can be shaped into one regular loaf, these round, knotted rolls make a lovely gift at any time, especially when paired with a decorative jar of honey and a few fresh autumn apples.

2	teaspoons dry yeast
1½	cups lukewarm water
2	eggs plus 1 egg yolk
¼	cup vegetable oil
½	cup honey
2½	teaspoons salt
3	cups whole-wheat flour
4–5	cups unbleached white flour
1	cup golden raisins (optional)
½	cup honey for drizzling

In a large bowl, sprinkle the yeast over the lukewarm water. Set aside for 5 minutes, until dissolved. Beat in eggs, egg yolk, oil, honey, and salt. Stir in whole-wheat flour and beat to a thick batter. Add white flour, one cup at a time, until mixture forms a medium-soft but not-too-sticky dough.

Turn out onto a lightly floured surface and let rest for 10 minutes. Have an additional cup of flour nearby in a small bowl. Once dough has rested, begin kneading. If dough begins to stick to your hands, flour your hands lightly. Knead for 8 to 10 minutes, until dough is smooth and stretchy.

continued ❧

Turn dough back into the mixing bowl, cover with a damp towel or plastic bag, and let rise in a warm, draft-free place for 1½ hours, or until doubled in bulk. Punch down and turn out onto a lightly floured surface. Knead for 2 or 3 minutes. At this point, depending on your schedule, you can let it rise again for another hour, or you can proceed directly to shaping the knots.

To shape the knots, pat the dough into a large rectangle. Sprinkle the golden raisins, if using, evenly over the dough, and roll up like a jellyroll. Now, break off a chunk of dough about the size of a small orange. Roll and stretch this hunk of dough between your palms until it forms a rope approximately 8 to 10 inches long. Loop the rope around itself and tie into a knot, pushing the end up through the middle of the knot. The roll will end up round, looking somewhat like a cinnamon bun. Place on a parchment-lined baking sheet, and repeat with the remaining dough. Make sure to leave room between the rolls for rising. (You'll probably need two baking sheets.)

Place rolls back in that warm place and let them rise until nearly doubled, approximately 45 minutes.

Preheat oven to 350°F. Drizzle each roll with honey. (This is easiest to do if you use a honey bear or other squeezable container, but you can also drip it off a spoon. Don't pour it straight out of the jar, however, because you might end up drenching the whole pan.) Bake for 30 to 35 minutes, until rolls are deep golden brown. Remove to a rack to cool.

{ yield: 10 rolls }

✳ ✳ ✳ ✳ ✳

elvis's favorite

Peanut butter and honey are one of those made-in-heaven combinations, especially if you use an all-natural, unsweetened peanut butter. In fact, it's food fit for a King—which is why we've dubbed this messy (but delicious!) sandwich the Elvis's Favorite, after his penchant for fried peanut-butter-and-banana sandwiches.

----

1   tablespoon butter

2   slices white or whole-wheat bread

2   tablespoons chunky peanut butter, preferably all-natural (see note)

1–2 tablespoons honey, or to taste

1   banana, peeled

Butter both slices of bread. Spread peanut butter on the unbuttered side of each slice. Top peanut-butter side of first slice with a drizzle of honey and as many banana slices as will fit. Drizzle on a little more honey and top with second slice of bread, peanut-butter-side in. Fry sandwich in a nonstick pan until golden on both sides, carefully flipping once. Transfer to a plate, cut in half diagonally, and serve hot.

{ **yield:** 1 sandwich }

note: It might seem a little ridiculous to insist on an all-natural, peanuts-only brand of peanut butter for this kind of sandwich. But it's a matter of taste: sweet, super-smooth processed peanut butters don't provide enough contrast to the bananas and honey in this sandwich. It's easy to identify a natural peanut butter: just check the ingredients to find one that lists only peanuts (and salt, if you prefer a salted peanut butter).

fat elvis, french elvis, and more

Some people shudder at the thought of bacon and peanut butter. Others think bananas are for wimps and insist that nothing goes better with peanut butter than a couple of slices of crisply fried bacon. If you want to go all the way, replace the bananas with bacon, leave off the butter and fry your sandwich in the leftover bacon grease (the Fat Elvis). Going back to the peanut-butter/banana combo, you could also substitute Nutella, a French chocolate-and-hazelnut spread, for the peanut butter (the French Elvis), or put Nutella on one slice of bread, peanut butter on the other (the Jerry Lewis). The possibilities are endless . . . but if you start eyeing the cabinets and wondering what sardines in mustard sauce might taste like with bananas and honey, it's time to have a glass of milk and go to bed.

* * * * *

ginger~honey soda

Back in the 1800s, a drink called "switchell"—water sweetened with honey and flavored with homemade apple-cider vinegar—soothed many parched throats during long, dusty summer days. Here, lemon and lime juices add a tropical tang to our updated version of this favorite summer cooler.

---

for the syrup

4	ounces fresh ginger (a 6-inch piece of gingerroot)
2½	cups water
1	cup honey
2	tablespoons lime juice
2	tablespoons lemon juice

Ice

Seltzer or sparkling mineral water

Lime or lemon wedges

Peel ginger and cut into thin julienne strips. Simmer ginger in water, covered, for 15 minutes. Remove from heat and add honey. Let steep, uncovered, for 20 minutes. Strain, pressing ginger solids against strainer to extract as much liquid as possible. Discard solids. Add lime and lemon juices to ginger liquid. Let cool, then pour into a clean bottle and refrigerate. To make soda, fill a tall glass with ice. Pour in ½ cup of syrup and top with sparkling water. Stir and garnish with a wedge of lemon or lime.

{ **yield:** 4 cups syrup, enough for 8 servings }

* * * * *

hot honey lemonade

Flannel jammies, a stack of magazines, and a big mug of hot honey lemonade: that's our answer to winter's annual siege of colds and flu. This comforting, delicious brew is full of cold-busting vitamin C, with plenty of honey to soothe a sore throat. If you live in an area where Meyer lemons thrive, use them to make an extra-sweet and fragrant drink.

2	lemons
3–4	whole cloves
2	tablespoons honey, or to taste
1	cup boiling water
1	cinnamon stick

Squeeze juice of 1 lemon into large mug. Slice second lemon very thin. Poke cloves into a lemon slice, and drop slices into mug. Add honey. Fill cup with hot water, and stir with cinnamon stick until honey has dissolved. Taste for sweetness and add more honey as necessary.

{ **yield:** 1 drink }

note: In a pinch, you can make this drink with bottled lemon juice. Use 2 tablespoons of lemon juice, and increase honey to 2½ tablespoons, as bottled juice is more bitter than fresh.

honey hot toddy

A sure chill chaser! Add 1 to 2 tablespoons dark rum or whisky along with the hot water.

morning elixir

Stir 2 teaspoons raw honey and 1 tablespoon unfiltered apple-cider vinegar into 1 cup of warm water. Drink every morning upon rising.

smoothie trio

Everyone loves a smoothie. And these three are the real thing—packed full of refreshing, healthy fruit lightly sweetened with a dab of honey. Smoothies also offer a great way to disguise the rather bitter taste of bee pollen. Just add a ½ teaspoon or so to any of these recipes, and buzz away!

bee happy

1	ripe banana, peeled
1–2	teaspoons honey
1	cup fresh orange juice
4–5	fresh or frozen strawberries
4–5	ice cubes
⅓	cup lowfat or nonfat plain yogurt
	Juice of half a lemon (optional)

Toss banana, honey, orange juice, strawberries, and ice cubes into the blender. Blend until smooth and frothy. Add yogurt and blend for a few more seconds. If it needs a little more oomph, add lemon juice.

{ **yield:** 1 drink }

blackberry bramble

. . . .

1	kiwi, peeled
	Small handful of ripe fresh or frozen blackberries
1	tablespoon honey
1	cup cranberry juice
4–5	ice cubes
1/3	cup lowfat or nonfat plain yogurt

Toss kiwi, blackberries, honey, cranberry juice, and ice cubes into the blender. Blend until smooth and frothy. Add yogurt and blend for a few more seconds. Pour into a tall glass.

{ **yield:** 1 drink }

nectar supreme

. . . .

1	cup apricot nectar
1	fresh ripe peach or 2 fresh ripe apricots, pitted
	Juice of one lemon
1–2	teaspoons honey
1/2	cup orange juice
4–5	ice cubes

Blend all ingredients until smooth and frothy.

{ **yield:** 1 drink }

✳ ✳ ✳ ✳ ✳

easy honey mustard

Back in the mid-eighties, flavored mustards suddenly became THE trendy food item. I'm still recovering from the chocolate-fudge entry I had to sample as a judge at a local mustard tasting. But while the raspberry-jalapeño mustards have, thankfully, disappeared, honey mustard has become a staple on sandwich menus everywhere, and with good reason. True honey mustard has a mellow tang that offsets this condiment's typical bite—just right on a slice of sharp cheddar, perfect on a sandwich of Black Forest ham. Try this version, and you'll never pack a picnic basket without it again.

½	cup smooth Dijon mustard
2	tablespoons full-flavored honey
1	tablespoon apple-cider vinegar
	Salt to taste
	Pinch of allspice

Mix mustard with honey, vinegar, salt, and allspice. Adjust seasonings to taste. Let mellow for a few hours in the refrigerator before using.

{ **yield:** approximately ¼ cup }

✳ ✳ ✳ ✳ ✳

honey spreads

These three spreads make a delightful change of pace from jam or plain honey. Packed into small decorative dishes, they are a pretty addition to a breakfast or tea table. Since the honey is not heated, all of its flavor will come through in the spread, so be sure to use a good-quality honey that will complement the flavorings—orange blossom or clover honey in the orange honey butter, for example, or chestnut honey in the hazelnut spread.

orange honey butter

Zest of one orange, finely grated (tangerine zest may also be used)

2 tablespoons honey

½ cup unsalted butter, softened

Whip zest, honey, and butter together with a wooden spoon or handheld electric mixer. When thoroughly amalgamated and smooth, pack into a small bowl or butter dish. Chill, covered.

hazelnut honey spread

1 cup hazelnuts

2 tablespoons honey

2 tablespoons grated bittersweet chocolate (optional)

Preheat oven to 350°F. Spread hazelnuts out on a baking sheet. Place in the oven for 6 to 8 minutes, until hazelnuts smell toasty and are just beginning to color. Remove from oven and rub hazelnuts in a clean dishtowel to remove brown skins. When nuts are bare, chop them very finely (or use a blender or food processor) until they form a nubbly paste. Stir in honey. For a chocolate-hazelnut variation, stir in the grated chocolate.

pistachio honey spread

1 cup unsalted shelled pistachios

2 tablespoons honey

¼ teaspoon rosewater

Chop pistachios very finely or grind to a paste in a food processor or blender. Stir in honey and rosewater.

venetian spiced honey preserves

Honey has a particular affinity for spices, especially warming ones like cinnamon, allspice, and cloves. Because Venice was a crossroads of trade, especially with the Arab nations to the east, this richly flavored honey, steeped with citrus and spices, always seems as if it would be right at home on the breakfast table of a merchant prince. Combining the honey with lemon and pectin turns it into a neat and tidy jelly—an idea for which I am indebted to Helen Witty, author of *Fancy Pantry* and *The Good Stuff Cookbook*.

for the spiced honey

3	cups honey
2	cloves
1	cinnamon stick, broken into pieces
3	allspice berries
6	black peppercorns, cracked
½	teaspoon dried lavender flowers
	Grated zest of one orange
	Grated zest of one lemon
¾	cup water
3	tablespoons lemon juice
3	ounces liquid pectin

To make the spiced honey, pour 2 cups of the honey into a large, clean jar or quart-sized glass measuring cup. Place in a saucepan half-filled with water. Bring water to a simmer. While water is heating, wrap spices and lavender flowers in a small square of cheesecloth, or place in a metal tea ball or reusable cloth teabag. When honey is warm, add orange and lemon zests and the spice bag. Keep water simmering over low heat for 20 minutes. Turn off heat and let honey steep surrounded by the warm water for another hour, then remove spice bag from the honey.

In a large saucepan over medium heat, combine 2 cups spiced honey, 1 cup plain honey, water, and lemon juice. When the mixture is bubbling, add the pectin. When the mixture comes to a full, rolling boil, set a timer and boil for 1 minute. Remove from heat. Set aside for another minute. Skim off any foam on top and pour into clean, sterilized jars. Leave ¼ inch of headspace on each jar, and top with clean, new lids and clean screw-top rings. Screw on caps firmly. If desired, place jars in a boiling water bath and boil for 10 minutes. Remove from water and let cool without disturbing for several hours, until jars are cold and lids are firmly sealed down. Sealed jars should be kept in a cool, dry place. Any preserves whose jars fail to seal should be refrigerated and eaten promptly.

{ yield: 4 cups }

note: You don't have to go all the way in making this spread. On its own, the flavored honey makes a delicious topping for hot biscuits. It's also very useful for adding extra flavor to poached fruit (see Faye's Honey Compote, page 86).

* * * * *

honey~almond chews

Honey gives a luscious edge to these chewy little confections of toasted almonds and candied ginger. Packed in layers of glassine paper or wrapped individually in colored plastic wrap, they make a lovely (and irresistible) gift during the holidays. Resist the urge to sample until the candy has cooled down—since the syrup must be boiled to the soft-crack stage (280°F), it's easy to burn your fingers or your tongue by sneaking a taste while it's still hot.

1	tablespoon candied ginger (optional)
2	cups sliced almonds or chopped walnuts
1	cup honey
½	cup sugar

continued ●▶

Preheat oven to 350°F. Lightly grease an 8-by-8-inch baking pan. Set aside. If using candied ginger, grind in blender or food processor until finely minced. Spread sliced almonds or chopped walnuts on a baking sheet and toast in the oven for 8 to 10 minutes, or until the nuts are pale golden and give off a toasty aroma. In a heavy-bottomed pan over medium heat, combine honey and sugar. Heat, stirring, until sugar dissolves, 8 to 10 minutes.

Add nuts and ginger, if using, and continue cooking, stirring frequently, until mixture turns a deep golden color and registers 280°F on a candy thermometer. Pour carefully into oiled pan, spreading in a thin (½-inch) layer. Score into small squares with a sharp knife. When cold, break into squares and store in airtight containers.

{ **yield:** approximately 36 pieces }

* * * * *

faye's honey compote

At my grandmother's house, no holiday dinner was complete without a bowl of compote: made from dried peaches, apricots, pears, and prunes poached in a light honey-sweetened syrup. At the time, I was more interested in the boxes of chocolate she kept hidden away in the sideboard, but now I love this dish not only for dessert but as an accompaniment to steaming oatmeal and a pot of hot tea on wintry mornings.

4	whole cloves
1	lemon, quartered, with seeds removed
3½	cups water
⅔	cup honey, or to taste
1	cinnamon stick, broken into three pieces
2	star anise pods, 4 allspice berries, or 6 whole black peppercorns (optional)
1	pound mixed dried fruit, such as peaches, apricots, prunes, raisins, pears, and/or apples

continued ◀▸

Insert cloves into one lemon quarter. In a large saucepan over medium heat, bring water, honey, lemon quarters, and spices to a simmer. Let simmer for two minutes, then add fruit. Let mixture come back to a simmer, then turn down heat to low and let simmer for 10 to 15 minutes, until fruit is tender but not mushy. Remove from heat and let cool in syrup. Remove spices and lemon quarters. Serve warm or chilled, with a little syrup ladled over each portion.

{ yield: 4 cups }

spiced honey compote

If you've made the spiced honey part of the recipe for Venetian Spiced Honey Preserves on page 84, you can substitute it for the honey in this recipe, leaving out or reducing the spices to taste.

✳ ✳ ✳ ✳ ✳

aunt rose's honey cake

This cake has a long pedigree. My friend Miriam Wolf, who grew up in Cheyenne, Wyoming, got this recipe from her mother, Dorothy Wolf, who in turn learned it from her own mother's sister, known as Aunt Rose. Aunt Rose's secret? Using a whole apple and orange (minus core and seeds), which gives this cake extra moistness and a lively texture.

½	cup oil
½	cup sugar
½	cup honey
2	eggs
1	small unpeeled apple, cored and chopped
1	small unpeeled orange, quartered and seeded
¾	cup strong brewed coffee or ½ cup strong brewed coffee and ¼ cup sweet wine (such as Manischewitz Concord grape or blackberry wine)
2	cups unbleached white flour

1½	teaspoons baking soda
½	teaspoon baking powder
½	teaspoon allspice
½	teaspoon cinnamon
¼	teaspoon ground cloves
¼	teaspoon salt
½	cup raisins

Preheat oven to 350°F. Line 2 loaf pans with parchment paper. Set aside. In a large bowl, beat oil, sugar, honey, and eggs together. Put apple and orange in blender or food processor and blend until finely chopped. Add coffee (or coffee and wine) to apple-orange blend. Sift flour, baking soda, baking powder, spices, and salt together. Add fruit mixture and sifted ingredients to the oil mixture in alternate thirds. Stir lightly after each addition until just blended. Stir in raisins. Pour batter into loaf pans. Bake until tester comes out clean, about 30 to 35 minutes. Cool in pans on a rack. Leave parchment on cake until serving.

Honey cake keeps very well. If possible, bake it the day before serving so the flavors have a chance to mellow.

{ yield: 2 cakes }

✳ ✳ ✳ ✳ ✳

baklava

Delicate pastries soaked in flavored honey syrups are a traditional specialty of many Middle Eastern cuisines. But the Greek baklava is perhaps the best known, with good reason—layers of rich nuts and crackling-thin golden pastry make it irresistible. Frozen phyllo dough can easily be found in the baked goods sections of most supermarkets—look for it next to the puff pastry and pie shells. Let it defrost overnight in the refrigerator, as frozen phyllo is brittle and more apt to crumple and crumble. While assembling your baklava, always keep a damp cloth over the bulk of the sheets to keep them from drying out.

continued ●▸

½   pound phyllo, defrosted

2   cups walnuts, blanched almonds, or pistachios, or a mixture of all three, finely chopped

2   tablespoons sugar

2   tablespoons honey

     Pinch of salt

     One of the following flavorings: 1 teaspoon grated orange and ½ teaspoon ground cardamom; 1 teaspoon cinnamon and a pinch of ground cloves; 1 teaspoon rosewater; 1 teaspoon orange flower water

½   cup butter, melted

for the honey syrup

¾   cup sugar

1¼   cups honey

1   tablespoon lemon juice

¾   cup water

     One of the following flavorings: 1 tablespoon grated orange rind; 1 stick cinnamon or ½ teaspoon ground cinnamon; 1 tablespoon rosewater (optional)

Preheat oven to 325°F. Lightly grease an 8-by-8-inch baking pan. Unfold phyllo dough and cut into 8-by-8-inch squares. Cover sheets with a damp cloth. In a small bowl, mix nuts, sugar, honey, salt, and your choice of flavoring.

Spread a phyllo sheet over the bottom of the baking pan. Using a pastry brush, lightly brush sheet with melted butter. Repeat with 5 more sheets, lightly buttering each sheet before adding the next. Spread approximately ⅔ cup of nut mixture over sixth phyllo sheet. Layer 4 sheets (buttering each one) on top of the nuts. Spread another ⅔ cup of the nut mixture on top sheet, and top with another 4 sheets (buttering between each one). Spread with last ⅔ cup of nut mixture. Top with 6 sheets, buttering each one and finishing with a final layer of butter.

Using a sharp knife, make four equal vertical cuts (about 1½ inches apart) through the top layer of pastry. Then make eight equal diagonal cuts (approximately 1 inch apart) across these strips to form 18 diamond shapes. (there will be a few trangular pieces left over along the edges—perfect for the cook to snack on before serving!) Bake for 30 to 35 minutes, until pastry is crisp and pale golden.

While baklava is baking, make the syrup. In a heavy-bottomed pan, heat sugar, honey, lemon juice, and water to boiling. Keep a close eye on it, as the syrup will froth and foam up. Add orange rind, cinnamon stick, or ground cinnamon, if using. Over medium-low heat, simmer for 10 minutes, until syrup has thickened slightly. If using rose water, add now. Remove from heat and pour into a pitcher. Let cool.

Pour cooled syrup over hot pastry. (Alternately, let pastry cool to room temperature before cutting. Reheat syrup to almost boiling, then pour hot syrup over cool pastry; (see note.) You may not need all of the syrup. Following the previously made cuts, cut pastry all the way through into diamonds and let syrup soak in for at least 3 hours before serving.

{ **yield:** approximately 16 pieces }

note: The trick to ensuring a crunchy, sticky pastry is to pour cool syrup over hot pastry, or hot syrup over cool pastry. As long as the pastry and syrup are opposite in temperature when they come together, you won't end up with soggy baklava.

a taste
of honey

Once you discover the wealth of wonderful honeys out there, you'll start finding all kinds of ways to use them in the kitchen. Here are a few of our favorites:

Fresh goat cheese drizzled with thyme honey, served with sliced green apples and toasted walnuts

Fresh blackberries swirled with clover honey over a dollop of vanilla yogurt

Buttered whole-wheat toast dripping with wildflower honey

Toasted hazelnuts, sharp sheep's milk cheese, and chestnut honey

Apple halves poached in apple cider, rum, and spiced honey

Lavender honey drizzled over ruby grapefruit halves, run under the broiler for a grapefruit brulee

Hazelnut-honey tartines: Hazelnut Honey Spread (page 83) spread on slices of toasted brioche

Fresh peaches sautéed in butter, honey, a sprinkle of allspice, and lemon juice, served over hot waffles

Buckwheat honey poured over buckwheat pancakes with country ham

chapter 6

crafting with
honey and beeswax

More flies are taken with a drop
of honey than a tun of vinegar.

Thomas Fuller,
Gnomologia

Fragrant honey soaps, soothing beeswax lip balms, honey-and-aloe hand creams: pick up just about any salve, moisturizer, lip balm, or cleansing cream, and chances are you'll find beeswax or honey on the ingredient list.

As a natural humectant, honey is a wonderful moisturizer for both hair and skin. Adding honey to your bath or making up a batch of honey cold cream or conditioner is a fun and easy way to enhance your well-being the natural way. Beeswax, has also been an important component of toiletries since Egyptian times; the versatility revealed by the recipes in this chapter is quite astounding. What other natural product can be used to soften chapped lips, polish fine furniture, and cast a flattering glow of candlelight over a party? With honey, beeswax, and a few other basic ingredients (all readily available in natural-food stores or art-supply shops), you can turn your bathroom into a spa and your kitchen into a craft studio.

However, as with any craft project involving heat or chemicals, safety should always be paramount. Wax can catch on fire if overheated. Never melt beeswax in a pot directly over an open flame. Always melt it in a double boiler or in a heatproof glass or metal bowl suspended over a pot of simmering water. (You can also melt wax in a glass bowl in the microwave.) Be very careful to avoid dripping hot wax on bare skin or clothing. If wax spills on the stove or near burners, turn off any open flame and mop or scrape up the wax immediately. Be careful to keep bits of grated or chopped wax from dripping onto the stove.

To avoid wax stains and make your cleanup a breeze, cover your work surfaces with several layers of newspaper. Once the project is complete, just bundle up the papers, and you're done!

Many of these recipes make great children's activities. However, children should be properly supervised at all times. Any melting or heating should always be done by an adult. Once removed from heat, melted beeswax congeals fairly quickly, but always be careful not to leave containers of hot wax in a spot where they can be easily tipped or knocked over.

✳ ✳ ✳ ✳ ✳

lip lickers berry gloss

This sweet, natural gloss is a treat for any age. Making this fruity pink gloss is an especially fun way for kids to get ready for an afternoon of dressing up. Just make sure to let the gloss cool to room temperature before using.

1	teaspoon sweet almond oil
12	fresh or frozen raspberries or blackberries
2	teaspoons honey

Combine almond oil, berries, and honey in a small glass or plastic bowl. Microwave for 30 to 60 seconds, until fruit has softened. Mash fruit with a spoon, then strain pulp through a fine sieve, discarding fruit seeds. Pour gloss mixture into small lip balm containers.

{ **yield:** 2 lip balms }

note: You can find sweet almond oil in the body-care section of many natural food stores

✳ ✳ ✳ ✳ ✳

bee balm

This easy-to-make lip balm tastes delicious and will keep your lips smooth and soft even in winter. Look for lip balm containers in health-food or crafts stores. Shops that specialize in soaps and lotions may also sell do-it-yourself empty containers.

1	tablespoon grated beeswax
2	teaspoons almond oil
1	teaspoon honey
12	drops orange essential oil

In a double boiler over simmering water, melt beeswax with almond oil and honey. When beeswax is completely melted, remove from heat and add essential oil. Stir and pour into small lip balm containers. Let cool. Cap when set and cooled to room temperature.

{ **yield:** 2 tablespoons, enough for 2 lip balms }

* * * * *

avocado~honey mud

Could your hair double as a tortilla chip after a fry-and-dry season of sun, swimming, and blow-drying? Skip the guacamole and turn your 'do silky soft with this luxurious mash of ripe avocado and humectant-rich honey.

1	avocado, peeled and pitted
⅓	cup honey
1	teaspoon lemon juice

Mash avocado in a small bowl. Stir in honey and lemon juice until well combined. Scoop onto clean, dry hair, spreading evenly from roots to ends. (Do this standing at the kitchen or bathroom sink, so any falling globs of avocado don't end up on your rugs!) Using a couple of bobby pins or clips, secure a plastic bag or plastic shower cap over your hair. Relax for 20 minutes, then rinse hair in warm water.

{ **yield:** 1 application }

✳ ✳ ✳ ✳ ✳

peppermint cooling cream

Sunburned or wind-chapped skin will appreciate this luscious cream, enriched with honey, beeswax, and lanolin and given a refreshing scent with peppermint.

⅓	cup water
2	teaspoons dried peppermint leaves (or 1 peppermint tea bag)
2	teaspoons dried chamomile flowers (or 1 chamomile tea bag)
⅛	teaspoon borax
2	tablespoons finely grated beeswax
⅓	cup olive oil
1	tablespoon lanolin
1	teaspoon honey
5	drops peppermint essential oil

Heat water to boiling. Place dried herbs together in a small bowl or cup. Pour boiling water over herbs and let steep for 5 minutes. Strain out herbs or remove tea bags. Dissolve borax in the liquid. Combine beeswax, olive oil, lanolin, and honey in a heat-proof glass or metal bowl or the top of a double boiler; heat over simmering water until beeswax is completely melted. Add borax mixture and stir until smooth. Remove bowl from heat. Add peppermint essential oil. Stir frequently as it cools—it should thicken and take on a creamy yellow color. To speed up the cooling process, place bowl in an ice-water bath. When cool, transfer to a clean, dry jar.

{ **yield:** approximately ½ cup }

✳ ✳ ✳ ✳ ✳

oatmeal~honey mask

Honey pulls in moisture while oatmeal flakes slough off dry, dead skin, leaving your face baby-soft and glowing.

3	tablespoons dry rolled oatmeal
¼	cup plain yogurt
1	tablespoon honey

Place oatmeal in a blender or food processor and grind very briefly, until reduced to a coarse powder. Empty powder into a small bowl and stir in yogurt and honey. Let stand for 5 to 10 minutes (so yogurt can soak into the oats). Smooth onto face (avoiding eye area) and relax for 5 to 10 minutes. Rinse off with warm water and pat dry.

{ yield: 1 mask }

✳ ✳ ✳ ✳ ✳

banana~honey mask

You might not be able to swing a vacation to Antigua this week. But relax with this creamy mask on your face, and you'll be rewarded by rehydrated skin that's as soft as a Caribbean breeze.

1	banana
1	tablespoon honey
2	vitamin E capsules

Mash banana and stir in honey. Prick vitamin E capsules and squeeze into banana-honey mixture. Smooth onto face (avoiding eye area) and relax for 5 to 10 minutes. Rinse off with warm water and pat dry.

{ yield: 1 mask }

✳ ✳ ✳ ✳ ✳

cleopatra's milk and honey bath

Just how did Cleopatra stay so mesmerizing? One story has her bathing in a huge marble tub filled with donkey's milk laced with honey. Try this modern version— while we can't promise that you'll end up lounging on a barge, your skin will definitely end up silky soft. This bath mixture should be made just before using.

1	cup powdered milk
4	tablespoons honey
2	tablespoons aloe vera gel

Mix all ingredients into a paste, adding a little hot water if necessary to dissolve milk powder. Drizzle into a hot bath. Soak and relax.

{ **yield:** enough for 1 bath }

✳ ✳ ✳ ✳ ✳

oshun's honey body scrub

For super-silky skin, try this honey-salt scrub, inspired by the Santeria deity Oshun. Powerful and extremely feminine, Oshun is a spirit of rivers and other "sweetwaters," and is often invoked when affairs of the heart need divine intervention. So bring a little love energy into your life by soaking in a warm bath, rubbing down with generous handfuls of this scrub, and rinsing your beautiful honey-scented skin with a quick shower. As with any salt-based scrubs, don't use on sensitive areas or around your eyes, nose, or mouth.

continued ●▸

1	cup coarse sea salt
½	cup Epsom salt
⅓	cup honey
1	tablespoon coconut oil
	A few drops of essential oil, such as sandalwood, ylang-ylang, or tangerine

Blend sea salt and Epsom salt. Mix in honey and coconut oil to form a moist scrub. Stir in essential oil. Use scrub on damp skin, paying extra attention to rough areas such as the feet and elbows. Rinse with warm water and pat dry.

{ **yield:** enough for 1 bath }

* * * * *

milk and honey soap

Call us chicken, but our enthusiasm for turning the kitchen into a home spa tends to shrivel once toxic chemicals are required. Making your own soap from scratch isn't rocket science, but it is chemistry, and one of the chief requirements is lye, the very caustic stuff responsible for all those red warning labels on Draino cans. However, you can still have a lot of fun personalizing your soaps without going back to Chem 101. In soapmaking terms, this is known as "rebatching," since you're starting out with ready-made soap, then adding your own favorite ingredients. This two-in-one bar doubles your bubbling pleasure with a creamy, lather-rich milk soap layered on top of a golden honey one. And you don't even need a special mold to make it. Just cut off the top of an empty quart container of milk, rinse it out, and voilà! Instant soap mold! (Of course, while researching sources, we did find a great company called Soapcrafters, based in Salt Lake City, which makes tons of cute soap molds, including a great hexagonal honeycomb-and-bee one. See Resources on page 116 for more information.)

Castile soap is a very gentle, pure soap usually made with mild saponified oils such as coconut or olive. Make sure the one you choose doesn't have any added fragrances or colorings, and is a pure vegetable-oil soap. Also, check the color before you buy, as some olive-oil soaps tend to be a murky greenish color. For best results, use a white or cream-colored bar.

for milk layer

1	4-ounce bar Castile soap, grated
1	tablespoon water
3	tablespoons powdered milk
2	teaspoons almond oil
1	teaspoon honey
	A few drops of vanilla essential oil (optional)

for honey layer

1	4-ounce bar Castile soap, grated
1	tablespoon beeswax, grated
2	teaspoons honey

If using plastic soap molds, rub interiors lightly with petroleum jelly. For the milk layer, in a large glass measuring cup placed in a pan of simmering water, melt grated soap and water until just beginning to go from sticky and clumpy to smooth. While soap is melting, in a small bowl, mix powdered milk, almond oil, and honey to a paste. Remove cup from heat. Stir in milk paste. Add a few drops of vanilla essential oil, if desired. Pour soap mixture into 2 plastic molds or milk cartons (see recipe introduction), filling each halfway. Let cool for 2 to 3 hours. When soap is fairly solid, make honey soap.

For the honey layer, in a large glass measuring cup placed in a pan of simmering water, melt grated soap and beeswax until just beginning to go from sticky and clumpy to smooth. Remove cup from heat. Stir in honey. Pour honey soap over milk soap layer in each mold. Let cool overnight. The next day, peel off carton or loosen from mold. Let cure on a rack for a few days. Soap should firm up, although it will remain softer than store-bought soap.

{ **yield:** 2 bars of soap }

✳ ✳ ✳ ✳ ✳

honey play clay

Squish it, squeeze it, smoosh it—you don't have to worry about the kids putting everything in their mouths when you let them mix up a batch of this easy-to-make, fun-to-use edible modeling dough.

1	cup peanut butter
½	cup honey
2	cups dry powdered milk

In a medium-sized bowl, mix peanut butter and honey together until smooth. Add powdered milk a little at a time until clay is thick and no longer sticky.

{ **yield:** approximately 3 cups }

✳ ✳ ✳ ✳ ✳

beeswax candles

Beeswax has been used to make candles for millennia. Easily molded or dipped, this pure wax produces a smooth, sweet-smelling candle that burns slowly and evenly. Beeswax stays solid even at relatively high room temperatures, so beeswax candles will rarely bend or lean in hot weather. Homemade beeswax candles are easy to make, and can be a lovely way to light up a dinner party or turn a birthday cake into something extra-special.

continued ❯

Remember, for safe candlemaking, never melt beeswax in a pot directly over an open flame; always melt it in a double boiler or in a heat-proof bowl suspended above a pot of simmering water.

Be careful not to drip hot wax on bare skin or clothing. If wax spills on the stove or near the burners, turn off the heat and scrape or mop up the wax immediately. Be careful to keep bits of grated or chopped wax from dripping onto the stove.

Most craft and art-supply stores offer several thicknesses of wicks from which to choose. The larger in diameter the candle, the thicker the wick should be. Use wicks specifically made for beeswax (as opposed to paraffin) candles. Do not use ordinary string or twine.

A tall, heavy glass jar with a wide mouth makes a perfect container for melted wax. If you don't have any quart-sized Mason jars on hand, many supermarket pasta sauces now come in similar tall glass jars. Enjoy a batch of pasta, then rinse and dry the jar. Since wax-coated jars can be hard to clean, save your jar for future wax projects, or just pop it into the recycling bin. Coffee cans look like they'd work well, but they're too light to stay put when placed in a pot of water. Even when filled with hot wax, they tend to bob around and tip over.

Always let wax set between dips when making dipped candles. Otherwise, the first layer of still-warm wax will bulge out beneath the next layer, resulting in a lumpy, uneven candle. Make sure your wax is completely cold and set before moving or unmolding a molded candle.

Before pouring wax from a hot container, slip a clean gardening or work glove over your pouring hand. It will protect your hand from the heat without the bulk of a potholder.

dipped birthday candles

....

1	pound beeswax
	Square braided wick, cut into 4- to 6-inch lengths (see note)

Chop beeswax into chunks small enough to fit through the mouth of a tall, heatproof glass or metal container. (Quart-sized Mason jars or empty glass pasta-sauce jars work well.) Place container in a pot of simmering water. Once wax is melted, turn off heat but leave container in hot water. Dip wick into melted wax for 45 seconds. Lift wick from wax, let cool for 10 seconds, and run your fingers down the length of the wick to straighten it. Let cool for 20 seconds. Dip back into the wax for a few seconds. Let cool for approximately 1 minute between dips. You can make several candles at once; while the first candle is cooling, you can dip the second, and so on. To free up your hands, suspend a strip of wood across two large jars or cans. Using a thumbtack or pushpin, pin wick to wood while cooling. For a small birthday-sized candle, 10 to 12 dips should be sufficient. As you dip, extra wax will run down the sides and lengthen the candle. If the candle grows too long to dip, pinch off this extra bottom wax and return it to the container. Repeat for as many candles as you like. Wrap finished candles in tissue paper and store in a cool, dry place.

> **note:** If you have a very large jar, you may need to use a longer length of wick to reach the wax inside. Use as much wick as necessary, then trim off the excess when the candle is finished.

molded candle

Glass, metal, and plastic molds in many shapes can be found in art-supply and craft-supply shops. Once you've chosen your mold, rub a few drops of liquid soap around the interior to make unmolding easy. (Be careful when using metal molds, as the edges can be very sharp.) For long, slender molds, drip a bit of soap on a tissue and poke it into the mold with a skewer.

2   pounds beeswax (for an average-size mold)

Wick (approximately 4 inches longer than length of mold)

Candle mold

Chop beeswax into small chunks. Melt in a heatproof glass or metal container over a pot of simmering water. Once wax is melted, turn off heat but leave container in hot water. Dip wick into melted wax for 45 seconds. Lift wick from wax, let cool for 10 seconds, and run your fingers down the length of the wick to straighten it. Thread wick through hole in bottom of mold so that unwaxed end will be at the open (top) end of mold. You should have approximately ½ inch of wick sticking out of the bottom of the mold. Take a small wad of soft wax and plug up wick hole on the outside of the mold. Straighten wick in the mold. Fill mold with hot wax. Make sure wick is centered in the mold. Holding a pencil horizontally above mold, twist excess wick around the pencil and lay pencil across mold to hold wick in place. Let cool until wax is cold and completely solid. Turn over and tap lightly to unmold. Trim bottom wick flush with base of candle.

floating seashell votives

Remember all those beautiful shells you found on the beach last summer? Now you can turn them into delightful floating votive candles, perfect for casting a romantic glow over an outdoor dinner party.

Beeswax (approximately 1 tablespoon, melted, per shell)

A selection of small, lightweight, shallow, rounded shells (scallop, clam, and mussel shells all work well)

Wick (approximately 2 inches per shell)

Cover a baking sheet with waxed or parchment paper. Chop beeswax into small chunks. Melt in a double boiler or in a heatproof glass or metal container over a pot of simmering water. As the wax melts, scoop out a small ball of soft wax. Stick this bit of wax to the rounded outer curve of the shell, forming a base. This way, the shell will not tip over when set down. Repeat with remaining shells. Set each shell onto baking sheet. Cut wick into 2-inch lengths. Dip a wick into melted wax for 20 seconds. Lift wick from wax, let cool for 10 seconds, and run your fingers down the length of the wick to straighten it. Bend wick to form an L shape, with the bare (unwaxed) tip up. Place L into shell, pressing bottom half of wick against shell to anchor it. Fill shell with wax. Repeat with remaining shells. Let cool until wax is solid. To use, float in glass bowl half-filled with cold water. Light and enjoy.

* * * * *

honeycomb candles

Sheets of beeswax foundation comb (available at crafts stores)

Wick (lengths approximately ½ inch longer than each candle)

Lay out one sheet of foundation comb. Line up wick about ¼ inch from the long edge of wax sheet. Using a hair dryer on a low setting, warm the wax gently until it can be rolled easily and will stick to itself when squeezed. Starting at the edge next to the wick, fold edge over wick and press firmly. Now roll tightly towards you, making sure wax stays warm and pliable. When fully rolled, press candle lightly between your palms to make sure it holds together. Repeat to make as many candles as you like.

spiral honeycomb candles

Slice one sheet of foundation comb diagonally to form two triangles. Lay wick along the long edge of one triangle. Fold edge around wick, then roll into a candle as above. Repeat for second candle.

✳ ✳ ✳
bibliography

Achaya, K.T. *Indian Food: A Historical Companion.* Delhi: Oxford University Press, 1994.

Avitabile, A. and Diane Sammataro. *The Beekeeper's Handbook,* 3rd ed. New York: Cornell University Press, 1998.

Battershill, Norman, et al. *Beeswax Crafts.* Tunbridge Wells: Search Press, 1996.

Brothwell, Don, and Patricia Brothwell. *Food in Antiquity.* New York: Frederick A. Praeger, Inc., 1969.

Coffin, Robert P. Tristam. *Mainstays of Maine.* New York: Macmillan, 1944.

Coleman, Mary Louise. *Bees in the Garden and Honey in the Larder.* New York: Doubleday, Doran and Co., 1939.

Collins, K.C., ed, and Lacy Hunter, ed. *Foxfire II.* New York: Anchor Books/Random House, 1999.

Corriher, Shirley. *Cookwise.* New York: William Morrow and Co., 1997.

Crane, Eva. *The Archaeology of Beekeeping.* New York: Cornell University Press, 1983.

Crane, Eva, ed. *Honey: A Comprehensive Survey.* New York: Crane and Rossak, 1975.

Davidson, Alan. *The Oxford Companion to Food.* Oxford: Oxford University Press, 1999.

Fisher, M. F. K. *The Art of Eating.* New York: Macmillan Publishing Co., 1990.

Frisch, Karl von. *The Dancing Bees.* New York: Harcourt Brace Jovanovich, Inc., 1966.

Graham, Joe M., ed. *The Hive and the Honeybee,* rev. ed. Hamilton, IL: Dadant and Sons, 1992.

Hubbell, Sue. *A Book of Bees.* New York: Random House, 1988.

———. *A Country Year.* New York: Random House, 1986.

Marks, Gil. *The World of Jewish Cooking.* New York: Simon and Schuster, 1996.

Morse, Roger. *A Year in the Beeyard.* New York: Charles Scribner's Sons, 1983.

———. *The Complete Guide to Beekeeping,* 3rd ed. New York: E. P. Dutton, 1986.

Morse, Roger, ed. *The ABC and XYZ of Bee Culture,* 40th ed. Medina, OH: A. I. Root Co., 1990.

O'Toole, Christopher, and Anthony Raw. *Bees of the World.* London: Blandford Publishing, 1991.

Roden, Claudia. *A Book of Jewish Food.* New York: Alfred Knopf, 1996.

Stelley, Diane. *Beekeeping: An Illustrated Handbook.* Blue Ridge Summit, PA: Tab Books, 1986.

Tannahill, Reay. *Food in History.* New York: Crown Trade Paperback, 1988.

Varro, Marcus Terentius. *On Agriculture.* London: William Heinemann, Ltd., 1934.

Virgil. *Eclogues and Georgics.* London: J.M. Dent and Sons, 1965.

Wigginton, Eliot, ed. *Foxfire 2.* New York: Anchor Books/ Doubleday, 1973.

Witty, Helen. *The Good Stuff Cookbook.* New York: Workman, 1997.

resources

mail-order honey

A. G. Ferrari
14234 Catalina Street
San Leandro, CA 94577
877.878.2783
www.agferrari.com

American source for Giuseppe
Coniglio and Daniele Devalle's
Sicilian and Tuscan honeys

Bosque Honey Farms
600 North Bosque Loop
Bosque Farms, NM 87068
505.869.2841
www.bosquehoneyfarms.com

New Mexico raw honey and
bee pollen

Candover Valley Honey Farm
2, Hackwood Cottages
Alton Road
Basingstoke, Hampshire
England, RG21 32BA
01256 329064

Cannon Bee Honey Company
6105 11th Avenue South
Minneapolis, MN 55417
612.861.8999

Basswood, buckwheat, and
clover honey from Minnesota

Cowboy Honey Company
P.O. Box 1387
Camp Verde, AZ 86322
520.567.3204

Mesquite honey from Arizona

Dean and DeLuca
2526 East 36th Street
Circle North
Wichita, KS 67219
877.826.9246
www.deandeluca.com

Gourmet food company selling
premium French, German,
Italian, and American honeys

Derwent Valley Apiaries
RSD 1268 Lyell Highway
New Norfolk, Tasmania 7140
03.6261.1764

Tasmanian leatherwood honey

Grossman Organic Farm
P.O. Box 1028
Tualatin, OR 97062
888.688.2582

Raw wildflower honey and
bee pollen from the Willamette
Valley

Guilmette's Busy Bees
5539 Noon Road
Bellingham, WA 98226
360.398.2146

Fireweed, raspberry, and wildflower honey from the Pacific
Northwest

Harold Curtis Honey Company
P.O. Box 1012
La Belle, FL 33975

Orange blossom, palmetto,
and mangrove honey

Hive Honey Shop
93 Northcote Road
London SW11 6PL
020.7924.6233

English honeys, honey-based
condiments, honey beauty
products, and honey-related
tableware

Honey Garden Apiaries
P.O. Box 189
Hinesburg, VT 05461
802.985.5852

Raw, unfiltered apitherapy
wildflower honey from
Vermont and New York State,
as well as wild-cherry raw-
honey cough syrup and
beeswax candles

Hunter's Honey Farm
3440 Hancock Ridge Road
Martinsville, IN 46151
765.537.9430

Raw wildflower honey from
Indiana, along with bee pollen
and beeswax candles

Marshall's Farm
P.O. Box 10880
Napa, CA 94581
800.624.4637
www.marshallshoney.com

Location-specific honey from
the San Francisco Bay Area
and the Napa Valley

McEvoy Ranch
P.O. Box 341
Petaluma, CA 94953
707.769.4122

Lavender-flower honey infused
with lavender from California's
Sonoma County

Plan Bee Honey
17 Van Dam Street
New York, NY 10013
212.627.0046
www.planbeehoney.com

New York State wildflower
honey, along with comb honey,
bee pollen, herb-infused honeys,
and gifts

River Hill Bee Farm
459 River Hill Road
Sparta, NC 28675
888.403.0392
www.riverhillhoney.com

Sourwood and wildflower
honey from the Blue Ridge
Mountains

**Tropical Blossom
Honey Company**
106 N. Ridgewood Avenue
Edgewater, FL 32132
386.428.9027
www.tropicbeehoney.com

Florida orange blossom, tupelo,
and saw palmetto honey, also
citrus honey with key lime and
tangerine essences

Uvalde honey
P.O. Box 307
Uvalde, TX 78802

Acacia (Huajillo) honey

crafting supplies

GloryBee Foods, Inc.
P.O. Box 2744
Eugene, OR 97402
800.456.4923
www.glorybee.com

Beeswax, candlemaking molds
and supplies, as well as honey
and beekeeping equipment

Soapcrafters, Inc.
2944 South West Temple
Salt Lake City, UH 84115
801.484.5121

Soapmaking supplies and molds

beekeeping books
and magazines

Avitabile, A. and Diane
Sammataro. *The Beekeeper's
Handbook,* 3rd ed. New York:
Cornell University Press, 1998.

Bonney, Richard. *Beekeeping:
A Practical Guide.* Pownell,
VT: Storey Books, 1993.

———. *Hive management:
A Seasonal Guide for
Beekeepers.* Pownell, VT:
Storey Books. 1991.

Flottam, Kim, ed. *The New
Starting Right with Bees,*
21st ed. Medina, OH: A. I.
Root Co., 1988.

Graham, Joe M., ed. *The Hive
and the Honeybee,* rev. ed.
Hamilton, IL: Dadant and
Sons, 1992.

Hubbell, Sue. *A Book of Bees.*
New York: Random House,
1988.

Morse, Roger, *The Complete
Guide to Beekeeping,* 3rd ed.
New York: E. P. Dutton, 1986.

———. *A Year in the Beeyard.*
New York: Charles Scribner's
Sons, 1983.

Morse, Roger, ed. *The ABC
and XYZ of Bee Culture,* 40th
ed. Medina, OH: A. I. Root
Co., 1990.

American Bee Journal
Published by Dadant and
Sons, Inc. 51 S. 2nd Street
Hamilton, IL 62341.
800.637.7468.
www.dadant.com

Bee Culture
Published by A. I. Root and
Sons, 623 W. Liberty Street
Medina, OH 44256.
800.289.7668.
www.airoot.com

To find a local beekeeping
club, try the source list at:
www.bee.airoot.com/
beeculture/who.html.
For general queries related
to honey and honey production, contact the National
Honey Board, 390 Lashley
St., Longmont, CO 80501.
303.776.2337.
www.nhb.org and
www.honey.com.

beekeeping and honey processing equipment

Bee Maid Honey
·625 Roseberry
Winnipeg, Manitoba
Canada, R2H 0T4
204.783.2240

Better Bee, Inc.
8 Meader Road
Greenwich, NY 13834
800.632.3379

BHC Honey Suppliers
Unit 3
Ffrwdgrech Industrial Estate
Brecon, Powys
Wales, U.K. LD3 8LA
01874 622335

Brushy Mountain Bee Farm
610 Bethany Church Road
Moravian Falls, NC
800.233.7929

Dadant and Sons, Inc.
51 South 2nd Street
Hamilton, IL 62341
800.637.7468
www.dadant.com

Fosse Way Honey
Northcote, Deppers Bridge
Southam, Warwickshire
England CV47 2SU
01926 612322

Garvin Honey Company
Avenue Three, Station Lane
Witney, Oxon
England, OX8 6HZ
01993 775423

GloryBee Foods, Inc.
P.O. Box 2744
Eugene, OR 97402
800.456.4923
www.glorybee.com

Hector's Apiaries Services
2297 Stanislaws Court
Santa Rosa, CA 95401
707. 579.9416

Judi's Farm Market
8020 Steveston Highway
Richmond, British Columbia
Canada, V7A 1M3
604.275.9535

Kidd Bros. Produce Ltd.
5312 Grimmer Street
Burnaby, British Columbia
Canada, V5H 2H2
604.437.9757

Mann Lake Ltd.
501 S. First Street
Hackensack, MN 56452
800.233.6663
www.mannlakeltd.com

Maxant Industries, Inc.
P.O. Box 453-S
Ayer, MA 01432
978.772.0576

A. I. Root Co.
623 West Liberty Street
Medina, OH 44256
800.289.7668
www.airoot.com

Ruhl Bee Supply
12713 NE Whitaker Way
Portland, OR 97230
503.256.4231

Western Bee Supplies, Inc.
P.O. Box 190
Polson, MT 59860
800.548.8440.
www.westernbee.com

* * *

table of equivalents

The exact equivalents in the following tables have been rounded for convenience.

liquid/dry measures

u.s.		metric
¼	teaspoon	1.25 milliliters
½	teaspoon	2.5 milliliters
1	teaspoon	5 milliliters
1	tablespoon (3 teaspoons)	15 milliliters
1	fluid ounce (2 tablespoons)	30 milliliters
¼	cup	60 milliliters
⅓	cup	80 milliliters
½	cup	120 milliliters
1	cup	240 milliliters
1	pint (2 cups)	480 milliliters
1	quart (4 cups, 32 ounces)	960 milliliters
1	gallon (4 quarts)	3.84 liters
1	ounce (by weight)	28 grams
1	pound	454 grams
2.2	pounds	1 kilogram

oven temperature

fahrenheit	celsius	gas
250	120	½
275	140	1
300	150	2
325	160	3
350	180	4
375	190	5
400	200	6
425	220	7
450	230	8
475	240	9
500	260	10

length

u.s.		metric
⅛	inch	3 millimeters
¼	inch	6 millimeters
½	inch	12 millimeters
1	inch	2.5 centimeters